It's All An  !

A study of the topic of illusion
as expounded in

A Course in Miracles, Buddhism,
Hinduism and other belief systems

Raveena Nash

TotalRecall Publications, Inc.

Houston   London   Toronto

ISBN: 978-1-59095-776-9

Printed in United States of America, Europe and Canada

TotalRecallPress.com
1103 Middlecreek Friendswood, Texas 77546
281-992-3131 281-482-5390 Fax

This book is dedicated to my son Adam,

with love and thanks for the cover photograph

It's all an illusion!

It's all an illusion!

It's all an illusion!

It's all an illusion!

It's all an illusion!

It's all an illusion!

It's all an illusion!

It's all an illusion!

It's all an illusion!

It's all an illusion!

It's all an illusion!

It's all an illusion!

It's all an illusion!

It's all an illusion!

It's all an illusion!

The Author

The author has been searching for meaning to life for nearly 25 years. During this period she studied scriptures and other books in her quest for enlightenment. Two years ago she was led to *A Course in Miracles* (*ACIM*), which caused her to do a 180-degree turn in her beliefs and in her perspective on life. She studied the course on a daily basis, one lesson a day for 365 days. She also studied the *Text* and *Manual*. She attended workshops and read several *ACIM*-related books. The central theme of ACIM is that the physical body and the world of form are illusions. Only the spirit is real and only the spirit has been created by God. She decided to write a book about her experiences with *ACIM* and to compare this belief system with others. Her major goal in life now is to awaken from the illusion and help others to awaken too.

She has a London University Honours degree in economics and her first job was as a mathematics teacher in a secondary school. Then she left teaching for a while and went to work in the media for around 16 years. She lived overseas at the time, working in the field of radio and television news. She also spent four years writing articles for a weekly newspaper. Raveena is interested in esoteric philosophy and holistic healing and she is a trained Reiki and Reconnective Healing practitioner. At present, she works in a secondary school teaching children who have learning and behavioural difficulties.

Foreword

This book is for all those who are searching for meaning in life. For those who are trying to make sense out of a seemingly meaningless world. For those who ask themselves: What is it all about?

This book is also for those who have picked up the self-study course entitled *A Course in Miracles (ACIM)* and then put it down because what it is saying is just too difficult for them to believe, or because what it is saying is unsubstantiated by other belief systems.

In writing this book I am hoping to show the reader that the teachings of *ACIM* are not that inconceivable or far-fetched and that there are many sages around the world whose teachings are very similar.

I am a student who has spent many years searching, studying and groping in the dark for a light to switch on that would make it all clear to me. I found that light not so long ago when I began to study *A Course in Miracles*. If I am able to share some of that light with others, then I will be honoured and joyful and my life will finally begin to make sense to me.

So this book is about shedding a little light on what to me is the only thing that does make sense in this world around us— illusion!

Table of Contents

<u>Introduction</u>

Life has never made any sense to me. For years and years I have been asking myself: What is it all about? We are born, grow up, grow old, get sick and die. Not a very pleasant thing to think about. Oh yes, there are many happy moments. Completing one's education, having a successful career, getting married, having children, looking after a loving pet, going on an exotic holiday, etc. The list is quite a long one but does any of it ever last? Is there anything enduring on this planet? I don't think so. I certainly have not found anything that could ever be taken to be permanent (with the exceptions of certain kinds of love—e.g., unconditional love, mother/child love.)

I have spent many years of my youth falling in and out of love and often wondered why that the "over the moon" feeling never lasted very long. Where did the passion go? Where did the love go? Maybe there was no real love involved at all—just physical attraction. How could true love die I asked myself? And why does everything come to an end?

Then years later, I became aware of two things. Firstly, that love—true unconditional love—never dies. And secondly, although everything does come to an end eventually, the death of the physical body is most definitely not the end of life because spirit is the only true form of life.

I also realised that life as we know it on the physical plane is not something one can be particularly optimistic about. How can we be optimistic about life if we are looking for permanence where there can only ever be impermanence? If we are looking for something or someone out there to make our own lives meaningful? That thing or person does not exist.

Before I stumbled upon *A Course in Miracles* (ACIM), I thought, after years of research, that I had finally discovered what life was all about. I believed in karma and reincarnation, in the evolution of the soul and in the ultimate need to return to Source/God. And God, to me, has always been a God of love and compassion. I have never been able to accept the belief that He is a God of retribution and wrath. Today, although I feel that karma and reincarnation are still a reality in the earth plane and I most definitely still believe in a God of love, many of my other beliefs have been turned upside down.

I had a vague understanding of the concept of *maya* (illusion or ignorance), which, according to the yogis, places a veil between humanity and reality. However, it was only when I studied *ACIM* that I appreciated the true extent of the illusion in which we are immersed. I think it is true to say that the idea of illusion is at the very heart of the teachings of *ACIM*. *"The world is an illusion. Those who choose to come to it are seeking for a place where they can be illusions, and avoid their own reality."* [1]

For us in the Western world, where there is so much emphasis on material well-being, youth, good looks and a wonderful body, and accumulating wealth, as well as an acute awareness of the ticking of the hands of time, the topic of illusion is undeniably an abstruse concept that is very difficult to come to terms with. Therefore, the message of *ACIM* is indeed a radical one. So I hope the reader will keep an open mind as he travels through this study on illusion. As *ACIM* points out, *"To learn this Course requires willingness to question every value that you hold. Not one can be kept hidden and obscure but it will jeopardize your learning."* [2]

There will be times in this book when I repeat important concepts of *ACIM*. This is because, as all teachers know, the only way to really learn something is to hear it over and over again. The repetition of key ideas is a technique that is employed quite frequently in *ACIM*, and since this book is a study of the teachings of *ACIM*, it would be very difficult not to do the same.

Raveena Nash

London

Summer 2008

---

[1] *ACIM* Workbook for Students (W) 291.
[2] *ACIM* Text (T) 299.

Chapter 1

A Course in Miracles—Illusion

"There is no life outside of Heaven. Where God created life, there life must be. In any state apart from Heaven life is illusion." [3]

As just mentioned, I have always believed that God was a God of love. Yet, gazing out of my window one day I noticed an elderly woman, all hunched up, walking along very slowly and obviously in pain. I asked myself, *"How could God allow us all suffer so much when we grow old?"* So many religions emphasise that He is compassionate and merciful. Yet, if you look at the ageing process itself, you cannot but realise that it is, in fact, very harsh and entails, for many people, a lot of suffering. Then, at its very end, life it can be painful, tragic and even humiliating.

If we switch on the TV news, yet again we are bombarded with all manner of suffering: destitution, famine, disease, disability, violence, war, terrorism, loneliness, cruelty to each other and to animals, destruction of the environment, natural catastrophes—it's a never-ending list. And furthermore, there seems to be no means of escaping from it all. History seems to be repeating itself over and over again ad infinitum. But how can all these horrific aspects of life on earth be reconciled with a God of love? The simple answer is that they cannot be.

Chatting to an atheist friend one day, I asked him why he was an atheist. "Look around," he said, "The world is such a cruel and harsh place. How on

---

[3] *ACIM*, T493.

earth could I believe in God?" And sadly I had to admit that what he said made sense.

But what if God is not responsible for the horrific things we see on our planet? What if He has nothing to do with them at all? What if all these things are not really happening but are only perceived by us to be taking place? What if...?

Well that is exactly the message of *A Course in Miracles (ACIM.)* This meaningless world of ours was *not* created by God. *"God did not create a meaningless world."* [4] God is perfect; God is eternal; God is unchanging; so how could He create a world that is far from perfect, exceedingly transient and forever changing? He could not! Here, at last, is something that does make sense.

A large part of this book will be dealing with the rather radical viewpoint that God did *not* create this world and all that is in it. In fact, this world is just an illusion. And, although that may seem to be a radical belief to many of us in the West, these teachings are neither new nor radical to those who have studied Buddhism and, to a certain extent, Hinduism.

And now let me try and summarise as clearly as possible the theory of the creation of the world as expounded in *ACIM*. God, being eternal and perfect, created, as an extension of Himself, His Son, Christ, who is equally eternal and perfect. At that point only perfect oneness, or non-duality, existed. Christ brought into being extensions of Himself as new Creations. At this stage we are simply talking about spirit and mind. Nothing of any physical substance was created. And it is important to remember that non-duality still exists, as all the new Creations are one with each other and one with Christ and God in Heaven.

Then at some point, the mind of Christ's extensions split into a "right mind" and "wrong mind." The wrong mind portion, on an impulse, decided to try to go it alone, i.e., to try to live apart from God. (This is *the fall* that we read about in the Bible.) At that point, the wrong mind split into separate fragments and multiplicity occurred, as did the world of phenomena that we see around us and

---

[4] *ACIM*, W23, Lesson 14.

everything in it. The ego was created by the wrong mind and became a replacement for God.

"Into eternity, where all is one, there crept a tiny, mad idea, at which the Son of God remembered not to laugh. In his forgetting did the thought become a serious idea, and possible of both accomplishments and real effects...." [5] The tiny mad idea was the idea of the mind splitting off and wandering away from Heaven and into the world of form.

From then on duality was the name of the game. We now had a world where subject and object were distinct from each other. We saw ourselves apart from God; we even managed to forget that we were ever one with God and Christ and we became fearful and also guilty. Guilty because of our subconscious memory of having split from our Creator and fearful because the world we created was indeed something to be afraid of. The ego, not having any of the omnipotence or permanence of God, could only create a world that was lacking in all respects—a world where only impermanence and change were possible. Therefore, all around us we find growth and decay, health and disease, youth followed by old age, physical life followed by inevitable death.

Another thing to bear in mind is that the ego, in its quest for autonomy from God, actually believed it could vanquish God, create the world of form as a place of refuge and rule supreme. *"In its insanity it thinks it has become a victor over God Himself. And in its terrible autonomy it 'sees' the Will of God has been destroyed. It dreams of punishment, and trembles at the figures in its dreams..."* [6] No wonder we are immersed in fear and guilt.

But how could the mind "create" anything, if there is only the one Creator? It is explained quite simply in *ACIM*. As God created His extensions, they were empowered with His powers of creation. However, they didn't do such a good job and ended up "miscreating" instead of creating as perfectly as God did. *"Because of your likeness to your Creator you are creative. No child of God can lose this ability because it is inherent in what he is, but he can use it inappropriately by projecting. The inappropriate use of extension, or projection, occurs when you believe*

---

[5] *ACIM*, T586.
[6] *ACIM*, W467.

that some emptiness or lack exists in you, and that you can fill it with your own ideas instead of truth." [7]

A rather complicated concept that is vital to understand is that, although the "creation" of the world of form took place, it only took place *at the level of the mind and not in Reality.* That is, it appeared to us to happen but it didn't really. It's just like a dream. It's all an illusion.

Another way of looking at the topic of the illusion of the physical body is to remember that God is forever and is changeless. Whatever is from God is therefore also forever and changeless. We are "extensions" of God, so we too are forever and changeless. Therefore, the part of us that is not forever and that is subject to change (i.e., the physical body) cannot be real, cannot be Truth.

The Course expresses this idea evocatively: *"The world you see is an illusion of a world. God did not create it, for what He creates must be eternal as Himself. Yet there is nothing in the world you see that will endure forever. Some things will last in time a little while longer than others. But the time will come when all things visible will have an end."* [8]

But there is hope for us in this world of illusions because at the very time of the "splitting of the mind," God created the Holy Spirit, who remains in our subconscious memory to help us return to our former reality. The Holy Spirit, referred to as the Voice for God in *ACIM*, is available to all who are ready to follow him back Home. Jesus is the manifestation of the Holy Spirit. I hasten to add that *ACIM* is not a Christian teaching and it stresses that the Holy Spirit is *not the only way back to God.* However, it is supposed to be a much quicker way than other Paths.

"Since you believe that you are separate, Heaven presents itself to you as separate, too. Not that it is in truth... Father and Son and Holy Spirit are as One, as all your brothers join as one in truth. Christ and His Father never have been separate, and Christ abides within your understanding, in the part of you that shares His Father's Will. (i.e., the "right" mind.) The Holy Spirit links the other part—the tiny, mad desire to be

---

[7] *ACIM*, Manual for Teachers (M) 17.
[8] *ACIM*, M85.

separate, different and special (i.e., the "wrong" mind)–to the Christ, to make the oneness clear to what is really one. In this world this is not understood, but can be taught." [9] So we can see that, if we are willing to learn, *ACIM* can teach us the Truth and show us the way Home. That is why I always find the *Course* to be uplifting and inspiring; just thinking about it puts a smile on my face.

That is a simplified version of the creation of the ego and the world of phenomena. However, a much more detailed and elaborate explanation is given in Gary Renard's outstanding book *The Disappearance of the Universe.* I strongly recommend this book to those who are interested in perhaps one day studying *ACIM* seriously. It is a wonderful introduction to the *Course.*

*"… Before, there was the perfect oneness of Heaven and nothing else. That is non-duality, or non-twoness. That is still reality. There is not **really** more than one thing, but now something different seems to be going on for you. There seems to be God **and** something else. That is the illusion of duality, and the world of multiplicity and the endless subjects and objects you perceive in it are merely symbolic of separation. While you may still try to create, you cannot really create without the power of God, so everything you make eventually falls apart"* [10]

Now that we are living in this dream world, we are at the mercy of the ego. And, as we will find out, the ego is not a very nice character at all. It is out for what it can get for itself, and all that it is aware of are lack, scarcity, fear, loss. So whenever we feel fearful or worried, we know that these feelings come from the very vulnerable ego that has set itself up in the place of God.

"The ego believes it is completely on its own… This is such a fearful state that it can only turn to other egos and try to unite with them in a feeble attempt at identification, or attack them in an equally feeble show of strength." [11] This is why we feel incomplete and seek to unite ourselves with others—partners, friends, family. And this is why we often feel like attacking others–people, nations, etc.

The ego can therefore be blamed for the chaos we see around us. We are not at peace within ourselves and can never be because in the world of form there's

---

[9] *ACIM*, T520.

[10] Gary Renard, *The Disappearance of the Universe,* p. 124, Hay House Inc., Carlsbad CA, 2004.

[11] *ACIM*, T58.

no escaping the ego and its delusional beliefs. As we cannot be at peace with ourselves, how can we ever be expected to live in peace with members of our family, community, society, country, world and universe? It cannot be—hence the breakdown of the family unit, the violence in our societies and all the conflicts and wars that have been waged in the past and that will inevitably continue to be waged in the present and in the future. So how do we get ourselves out of this mess? We awaken from the dream. We become aware of the whole crazy set-up of the ego and we strive to overcome it. It is no easy task but I will deal with that in Chapter 7.

One way of awakening from the dream is to choose God instead of the ego. We are told, *"Either God or the ego is insane. If you will examine the evidence on both sides fairly, you will realize this must be true. Neither God nor the ego proposes a partial thought system. Each is internally consistent, but they are diametrically opposed in all respects so that partial allegiance is impossible"* [12] If we choose God we consciously find a Path back home so that we can recover our original eternal nature of pure freedom and love. If we choose the ego instead, we close our minds off to the Truth and are content to go around and around on the wheel of life, alternating between pleasure and pain, from one life to the next, living a life of illusion in a world of illusion. There's not much of a choice really, is there?

The *Course* expresses it even more bluntly: *"Do you like what you have made?—a world of murder and attack, through which you thread your timid way through constant dangers, alone and frightened, hoping at most that death will wait a little longer before it overtakes you and you disappear.* **You made this up.***"* [13]

One should realise that the ego is extremely vulnerable as it was not created by God and therefore it has none of the strength of God within it, although the "right" part of the mind does. And that is why those in New Age circles believe that God is within us. He is, but not in the ego portion.

"The ego is idolatry; the sign of limited and separated self, born in a body, doomed to suffer and to end its life in death. It is the "will" that sees the Will of God as enemy, and takes a form in which it is denied. The ego is the "proof" that strength is weak and love is

---

[12] *ACIM*, T193.
[13] *ACIM*, T429.

fearful, life is really death, and what opposes God alone is true. The ego is insane. In fear it stands beyond the Everywhere, apart from All, in separation from the Infinite." [14]

We are reminded regularly throughout the *Course* that we are not bodies but we simply perceive ourselves to be so. *"Your reality is only Spirit."* [15] If we search for anything enduring through our physical form, we will not find it. Pleasure, indeed, we can feel, but only for fleeting moments. Good health we can achieve, but eventually, no matter how healthy our lifestyle is, disease and death will catch up with us. Those who do lead healthy lives are prolonging the time they spend being physically fit and active but they are not immune to the grim reaper. And sometimes even those who are careful about good nutrition, exercise, meditation, etc., succumb to dreaded diseases such as cancer and heart disease. Why is this?

"All sickness comes from separation. When the separation is denied, it goes. For it is gone as soon as the idea that brought it has been healed, and been replaced by sanity." [16] This is why one of the lessons of the Workbook tells us, *"Sickness is a defence against the truth....it is an insane device for self-deception....How do you think that sickness can succeed in shielding you from truth? Because it proves the body is not separate from you, and so you must be separate from the truth. You suffer pain because the body does, and in this pain are you made one with it."* [17]

In other words, the more pain we feel the more we will identify with our bodies and the less likely we are to identify with our true self, which is spirit. It's simply the ego making sure we don't awaken from its crazy, unreal world.

Have you noticed how people who have a health problem or pain somewhere in their bodies can't help but speak about it? I am as guilty of this as the next person. But since studying *ACIM* I try not to dwell on or to speak about any ailment or pain too much. I must admit though that it can be difficult at times if you have a splitting migraine! Funnily enough, at the exact time that I started to study the *Course* I developed a quite severe pain in the neck and I have it to this

---

[14] *ACIM*, W467.
[15] *ACIM*, T10.
[16] *ACIM*, T554.
[17] *ACIM*, W257 & 258, Lesson 136.

day, although some days it is less painful than others. I can't but help think that it is my ego fighting back as it sees me trying to turn away from it and to find the Truth. Well, it won't win!

Death follows ill health in the end for us all and it is not something we like to think about or mention in public. Yet, we all know that it cannot be avoided. The *Course* has taught me, however, not to fear death as I used to. If the body is unreal then the death of the body must also be unreal. Spirit cannot die.

*"And what is the black-draped body they would bury? ... The body no more dies than it can feel. It does nothing. Of itself it is neither corruptible nor incorruptible. It **is** nothing. It is the result of a tiny, mad idea of corruption that can be corrected. For God has answered this insane idea with His Own..."* [18] So a sick body is the product of a sick mind. If we can change our perceptions, this should translate into a healthy body.

Kenneth Wapnick was an associate of Helen Schucman and William Thetford, who were the scribes for Jesus' teachings in *ACIM*. He has been *ACIM* teacher since 1973 and has written many invaluable books on the subject. In his book *The 50 Miracle Principles of A Course in Miracles* he states with reference to Principle 24, *"The mind made up everything in this world. A Course in Miracles really means this in the all-inclusive cosmic sense of making up the entire physical universe. For our purposes here, it is saying that we made the body and the body's laws, which means we made the laws of sickness and we made the laws of death. Because we did that, we can change them."* [19]

The *Course* teaches us that there is no death and that the fear of death will be eliminated when we awaken from this illusory world. Death is no escape, so suicide is futile. The only way to escape from this world of form is to realise that it isn't there and follow the guidance of the Holy Spirit (or another chosen Path) back to God. There is no death in eternity.

I mentioned earlier that my friend said he was an atheist because all the suffering in the world made it impossible for him to believe in a loving God. In

---

[18] *ACIM*, W417 & 418.

[19] Kenneth Wapnick, Ph.D., *The 50 Miracle Principles of A Course in Miracles,* p. 66 Temecula, CA, 2005, used by permission of the *Foundation for A Course in Miracles.*

fact, *ACIM* actually mentions this. *"Death is the central dream from which all illusions stem. Is it not madness to think of life as being born, aging, losing vitality, and dying in the end? ... It is the one fixed unchangeable belief of the world that all things in it are born only to die. This is regarded as the 'way of nature', not to be raised to question, but to be accepted as the 'natural' law of life. The cyclical, the changing and unsure; the undependable and the unsteady, waxing and waning in a certain way upon a certain path—all this is taken as the Will of God. And no one asks if a benign Creator could will this. In this perception of the universe as God created it, it would be impossible to think of Him as loving. For who has decreed that all things pass away, ending in dust and disappointment and despair, can but be feared."* [20] And this is something that I have always found difficult to understand. How could a loving God create us human beings, endow us with the love of life and the instinct of self-preservation and then take it all away from us when the grim reaper comes calling? This has never made sense to me. I have also found it hard to believe that He could have created such vile things as deadly viruses, harmful bacteria, germ-spreading flies and mosquitoes! *Now I know He did not.*

In one of the sections of the Text, *ACIM* refers to the physical body as the "hero of the dream." This section describes the way we humans see ourselves at the centre of our little imaginary worlds and how we live a little and then die, buried amongst others who have lived and died. It really paints a rather bleak picture and is more like a nightmare than a dream.

"The dreaming of the world takes many forms, because the body seeks in many ways to prove it is autonomous and real. It puts things on itself that it has bought with little metal discs or paper strips the world proclaims as valuable and real. It works to get them, doing senseless things, and tosses them away for senseless things it does not need and does not even want..." [21] How true is that description! I can't help but smile rather ruefully as I think of all the clothes I have in my wardrobe that I hardly ever wear.

I remember hearing in a news report that people in the USA spend very long hours at work to make money and then spend most of their spare time spending

---

[20] *ACIM*, M66.
[21] *ACIM*, T585.

that money! It doesn't really make sense, does it? Although I would be the first to acknowledge that it is difficult to cut back on shopping when, in our consumer society, we are bombarded with advertisements left, right and centre, which make us feel we really need these "senseless things."

The travel industry makes us feel we really need to have a holiday abroad at least once a year; the food industry is always coming up with new convenience meals or special diet foods that we "really must have"; the fashion industry encourages us to throw away perfectly good clothes, sunglasses, shoes, handbags, etc., because they have now gone out of fashion and must be replaced; the hi-tech industry convinces us that our computers, laptops, mobile phones and mp3 players are all outdated and need replacing at least once a year; the housing industry urges us to renovate our homes and carry out loft conversions or build conservatories in order to increase the value of our homes; the automobile industry produces irresistible newer models of flashy looking cars every year, etc., etc., etc.

But is it really fair to blame all these industries? Can't we simply say, "No, I am not interested"? I think it is easier to do that when one has been around for a while and is no longer as caught up in the things of this world as one once was. But I don't think it is easy for young people today. We live in a consumer society and there's so much choice and variety out there; it is difficult to ignore it all.

Yet being a victim is something rather distasteful to me. I have always believed that we make our own reality. And the *Course* warns us, in one of the Workbook lessons, not to perceive ourselves as victims: "*I am not the victim of the world I see...The idea for today is a particularly useful one to use as a response to any form of temptation that may arise. It is a declaration that you will not yield to it, and put yourself in bondage.*" [22] That should encourage us not to go out and buy a new car, new hi-tech gadgets, new clothes, new garden furniture, etc., that we don't really need. I believe buying expensive items really does put us in bondage. It is taking me five years to pay for my car and I am really looking forward to the day when I won't have that extra monthly expense. It means I am tied to my job, as I have to make sure I can earn enough to pay for it. That is just one example. But the

---

[22] *ACIM*, W48, Lesson 31.

more valuable possessions one has, the more "in bondage" we become. We have to insure them; we worry about losing them; we have to store them if we go away for a while and we may delude ourselves into believing that accumulating valuable material possessions is what life is all about.

ACIM teaches us that the physical body (which we believe exists but doesn't) has only one function in our belief system and that is to be put to use to serve the Holy Spirit and in this way help bring about our salvation and the salvation of others. *"The Holy Spirit teaches you to use your body only to reach your brothers, so He can teach His message through you. This will heal them and therefore heal you."* [23]

An equally important function that we have while we appear to be in our physical bodies is forgiveness. In fact, I see *ACIM* as being the path of forgiveness because when we realise that everything in the phenomenal world is an illusion, then we realise that all human beings are simply puppets ruled by an illusory, vulnerable and grasping ego. We are therefore not really to blame for our selfish thoughts, words and deeds because we know no better. However, upon awakening and becoming more conscious individuals, we gradually begin to overcome the ego, maybe initially at the subconscious level, but later it will inevitably be at the conscious level too. So we forgive people who are selfish, unkind, cruel, etc., because we recognise all those traits in ourselves and because we know it is not really their divine inner portion (or the "right" portion of their minds) that is acting this way. (We also have to learn how to forgive ourselves.) We don't condone their deeds but we understand that they stem from the illusory ego and not from the divine spark within.

There's another way of looking at forgiveness. Since we made this whole world up and everything in it and it isn't really happening although it appears to be, then there's nothing to forgive. It may appear to be that someone offended me, stole from me, attacked me but in reality that never happened, so all I can do is be aware of this and realise that there is nothing to forgive. *"Forgiveness ends the dream of conflict here"* [24]

---

[23] *ACIM*, T157.
[24] *ACIM*, W469, Lesson 333.

There are at least two more aspects to forgiveness that will be dealt with in Chapter 9.

I would like to point out that *ACIM* teaches us at two different levels: at the metaphysical and at the practical or physical level. So concepts such as illusion, miracles, the eternal now, etc., refer to the metaphysical level. However, when the *Course* talks about linear time and choosing between the ego or the Holy Spirit, it is talking to us in terms that we, in our physical bodies, can comprehend, even though linear time, as we shall see in Chapter 6, does not really exist.

Now, let's take a look at some of the terminology of *ACIM*. Firstly, why is it called *A Course in Miracles*? It is because the miracle is the *change of perception* that takes place within us when we awaken to the fact that the world of the ego is an illusory world. By changing our perception and awakening from the dream, we gain in strength and are able to "heal" others as we have become healed. Healing here refers to healing the mind, not the body, and involves changing the erroneous perceptions of others just as we have changed our own. Thus *ACIM* is designed to bring about a gradual change in the way we look at the world of form. When this happens, a miracle has taken place.

"A miracle is a correction. It does not create, nor really change at all. It merely looks on devastation, and reminds the mind that what it sees is false. It undoes error, but does not attempt to go beyond perception, nor exceed the function of forgiveness. Thus it stays within time's limits. Yet it paves the way for the return of timelessness and love's awakening, for fear must slip away under the gentle remedy it brings." [25] Imagine a world without fear—that would indeed be a miracle. I should add that whenever we change our perception and forgive both ourselves and others, we are acting in a loving manner, and the outcome can only be peace and serenity. That is why it is stated, *"...fear must slip away"*. A miracle is an expression of love. And where there is love there can be no fear.

Another term one comes across quite frequently in *ACIM* is "Atonement." Atonement is closely linked to the concept of miracles and is a process involving a change of perception and forgiveness. Thus we realise this world is not real

---

[25] *ACIM*, W473.

and so we forgive those who have offended or hurt us in any way, and each time we do that a miracle has taken place. By forgiving others, we ourselves are forgiven and this is the process of Atonement. Our minds have now become healed. The following important sentence summarises this brilliantly, *"The miracle is the means, the Atonement is the principle, and healing is the result."* [26]

After I studied these concepts, I decided it was time to speak to a teacher of *A Course in Miracles.* So I went to Kensington Gardens in central London and met Ian Patrick, who is the manager and co-ordinator of the *Miracle Network*[27], which he established in 1994. He is the editor of the *Miracle Worker* magazine and has been a student and teacher of *ACIM* for many years. Ian has given workshops on the teachings of *ACIM* and has just written a book on the *Course.* I asked him firstly about the topic of illusion...

IP: Well I think it is a very challenging area for many people because they say things seem very real—you can touch things and feel things and so they believe they are living here. That's the whole essence of the *Course's* message—that we have totally bought into the illusion, so of course, by definition, we are going to think that this world is real and find it difficult to believe that it is a dream. In my workshops I make the analogy of our sleeping dreams. At night our dreams seem very real to us—the struggles and dramas that we dream about—but when we wake up we realise that it was just a dream and that it never happened. So it is exactly the same thing. This waking dream that we are living seems just that much more real than a sleeping dream, but it actually is no more real.

RN: So the body, the earth, time and space were all created by the ego at the time of the separation, the time of the splitting of the mind?

IP: Yes, the *Course* talks about the moment of terror when we believed that we had separated from God. In our experience, we left God and heaven and obviously felt incredibly guilty for doing that and the ego believes that guilt demands punishment so that was the origin of fear. We believed we were going to be punished for the separation, which, of course never really happened, but the ego believed that it did. So then it

---

[26] *ACIM*, T23.
[27] www.miracles.org.uk

created this illusory world as a place to escape from God's wrath. So in our experience—that is the experience of the collective ego, because initially there was just one—it was as if God was no longer there and as if heaven was no longer there. So we believed that we had destroyed heaven and in the process killed God.

RN: But the Holy Spirit remained there as the only link to God?

IP: Yes, remember that it is not true that we destroyed heaven and God. It is not possible that a part of "the all" could be separated like that. So there remains a link in our minds back to the truth.

RN: One thing I really like about the *Course* is its very clear-cut logic. So for example, if God is eternal, then everything He creates would have to be eternal like Him. If God is perfect, then we would have to be perfect. But we're not, as we can see from this world...

IP: Yes, I love the logic, which is totally the opposite of Christianity, which believes that God created the physical world. The *Course* says that God didn't create this physical world, because we could say God is perfect, eternal, infinite and changeless and this world is the opposite of that. God would only create like Himself and as this world is totally not like God, therefore he could not have created it. The logic is perfect and you can say "I don't believe it," but you can't actually argue against the logic.

RN: I call *A Course in Miracles* the path of forgiveness or the yoga of forgiveness. Why does forgiveness have this major role in the Course?

IP: Forgiveness undoes the illusion of separation if followed through fully. So if this world is an illusion and we are entirely innocent and still remain at one with God, our issues in this world and our grievances with other people are projections. If the world is an illusion it is neutral—an illusion can't be good or bad, it's simply nothing, neutral. But we project onto it and say, for example, "This person did a bad thing, they are wicked, or evil or selfish, etc." If we realise that that is simply our projection and we withdraw that from them, and realise that it is about something we've made up because we don't want to look at our own beliefs about ourselves, and then in turn realise that those beliefs about ourselves are errors, and ask the power of the Holy Spirit to help us undo the beliefs we have about ourselves, then He must do that. So, we realise our innocence and we have the experience of being at one with our brother in front of us and ultimately at one with God.

RN: So it is not forgiveness in terms of what is written in the Bible but more than that. It really means overlooking things because they never really happened, doesn't it?

IP: I think it goes beyond overlooking because overlooking means it's there, but we will overlook it and pretend it didn't happen. It's more about letting things go. It is often said that the starting point of forgiveness is to consider that it didn't actually happen. But in my experience if I can let it go and realise that this is just a projection that I have made and withdraw that and let it go, then I realise that it never really happened. So I realise that at the end of the process of forgiveness not at the beginning.

RN: It isn't always easy to tell yourself it didn't really happen; for example, if someone cuts you up when you're driving?

IP: Well, it is not that that didn't happen within the illusion of the world. It's what I made that mean. For example, if someone cuts me up in traffic, I could make that mean that the world is out to get me, that I'm a victim. But then you have to work at changing those beliefs.

RN: Another thing I like about the *Course* is that it has made me feel that enlightenment is a possibility for me one day and actually it says that enlightenment is inevitable for everyone and that this is just a dream we are having and in reality we are actually in heaven. Do you feel like that?

IP: Well, I think the word enlightenment to me can also mean a process of getting lighter. As I practice forgiveness, when I remember to on a day-to-day basis, then I get lighter because I am carrying around less guilt, less of a weight on my shoulders. I don't find forgiveness very easy to do. Of course the ego doesn't want you to forgive and so sometimes I forget to forgive for quite a while. But, yes, awaking is inevitable, because the *Course* says, in truth, we have never left Heaven, our true home.

RN: The *Course* says that if you turn to the Holy Spirit and practise forgiveness, you can wipe out thousands of years of what would otherwise have been a slow process of spiritual evolution, doesn't it?

IP: Yes, the *Course* is very black and white. You are either listening to the ego, which is totally untrue, or you are listening to the Holy Spirit, which is totally true. The path of the Course is gradually a process of listening more and more to the Holy Spirit and that is what it encourages you to do.

RN: I find it interesting that the *Course* does not lay down specific rules such as, for example, saying you should cut out things like wine, coffee, etc. The only thing you are expected to do is to listen to the Holy Spirit.

IP: Yes, you can eat meat; you can do whatever you want. It's great because it doesn't talk about any behaviour so long as you are not listening to your ego or so long as it's not guilt-inducing. You just ask yourself: "What am I doing this thing for? Is my ego going to use it for guilt?"

RN: The *Course* makes a distinction between "creating," which is what God does, and "making" or "miscreating," which is what the ego did when it made the universe as a place of refuge. Is this correct?

IP: Yes, that distinction is made—but what is important is how you see what's in front of you. If you are seeing it through your ego, then that is a "miscreation," but if you are extending love, then what you extend the love to becomes something you've created. The *Course* talks about God extending and the ego projecting. The projection is the negative use of the positive dynamic of extension.

RN: In one of his books Kenneth Wapnick, the well-known author and *Course* teacher, says that everything that is good and beautiful in the world was also made by the ego, not just the bad things. But, being a nature lover, I have a hard time coming to terms with the fact that the ego created things like a beautiful forest or classical music. How can we not like some of the beautiful things around us in the world?

IP: I think it is OK to like these things. The *Course* talks about the "echoes of God" and I think that includes such experiences as looking at a beautiful sunset, or listening to a nice piece of music, or looking at a painting, or whatever it is.

RN: So those sorts of things won't keep us trapped in the ego?

IP: No, because you can have a little bit of an experience of God whilst looking at a sunset or listening to a beautiful piece of music. Ken Wapnick turned to spirituality through listening to Mozart! I think the word "echo" is relevant because if you think of an echo, it is not the original sound; it is like a secondary thing. So when you are looking at a sunset, that's not God and it was not created by God, but the experience you have is like an echo of God. The other thing about nature is that we tend to be very selective about what we choose to see. If you look at plants, for example, the roots are actually trying to strangle one another! Also animals devour each other in nature, so it has a cruel and ugly side too. The truth is that it is neutral. It's neither beautiful nor ugly.

RN: And the thing to remember is that none of it is enduring.

IP: Yes, none of it will last. Only what God created will last.

RN: The *Course* talks a lot about "sin"; however, it does not have the same meaning as the "sin" mentioned in the Bible does it? I mean it is mainly an error in perception, isn't it?

IP: The original meaning of the word sin is "you have missed the mark" — it's an archery term. So we can think of it like that. We have just missed the mark; we made a small mistake.

RN: We are told in the *Course* to try to avoid fear and guilt, aren't we?

IP: Well, it is not really about avoiding. Fear is inevitable in this world. But it is about changing our mind about fear, about undoing the thoughts of fear. It's not about never being fearful nor about never being angry. The *Course* says anger is never justified but it doesn't say you are never going to get angry. What you have to do if you are angry is find a way of learning about the situation and using it as a means of forgiveness.

RN: One last question — did you find that when you first studied the *Course*, it turned all your beliefs upside down because it is quite radical, isn't it?

IP: Yes, it is radical and the *Course* talks about it being a complete reversal of the thought system of the world. You are asked to reconsider all your beliefs. However, in many ways the Course was coming home to me.

RN: It made sense to you?

IP: Well, it was more than that. It resonated with me. Some of the core ideas, for example, that only love is real—I knew that was true as a kid because I thought logically that God is the creator and God is love, so how can there be a Devil? How can there be evil? So when I read that only love is real, in the *Course*, I said, "Wow," this book is for me! And the Course's teachings on the crucifixion and resurrection also made sense to me

Chapter 2

Buddhism—Illusion

"All forms are unreal, he who knows and see this becomes passive in pain; this is the way that leads to purity. " [28]

In this chapter I would like to examine whether or not there is some similarity between Buddhist beliefs and those of *ACIM*. Although there certainly are differences, I believe that some comparisons can be made.

If we start with a look at the creation of the universe, an interesting parallel can be made between *ACIM* and the teachings of Chögyam Trungpa, a Tibetan meditation master. According to him, both open space, belonging to no one, and primordial intelligence have always existed. We [29] were one with this open space and intelligence and one with each other. There was no self-consciousness. But then something strange happened. *"We just became too active in that space. Because it is spacious, it brings inspiration to dance about; but our dance became a bit too active, we began to spin more than was necessary to express the space. At this point we became* **self-***conscious, conscious that 'I' am dancing in the space. At such a point, space is no longer space as such. It becomes solid. Instead of being one with the space, we feel solid space as a separate entity, as tangible. This is the first experience of duality–space and I."*

---

[28] *Dhammapada – A Collection of Verses from the Pali Canon of Buddhism*, p. 64, Chapter 20, verse 279, translated by F Max Muller, Red & Black Publishers, Florida, 2008.

[29] I am not too sure what he means when he says "we" because there is no belief in the spirit or the soul.

[30] So we can see that he explains that we began to "dance about" and at that point duality was experienced for the first time. This is really quite similar to the teachings of *ACIM*, which state that when the mind (that was an extension of Christ) split and became fragmented, duality occurred and the world of form was experienced.

The *Course* then says that when the separation occurred we forgot our divine origins and the ego tried to take the place of God. Trungpa says that after we experienced solid space as being tangible, *"Then a kind of blackout occurs, in the sense that we forget what we were doing. There is a sudden halt, a pause; and we turn around and discover solid space, as though we had never before done anything at all, as though we were not the creators of all that solidity."* [31] I find it really interesting that he clearly implies that we are the creators of the world of form, of solidity. That is the exact same teaching as *ACIM*.

On the next page in his book, Trungpa explains that following this, we refused to see the space as openness, as it originally was (I think this open space that he refers to can be compared to Heaven in *ACIM*.) So we completely ignored it and this is *avidya*, which means *ignorance*, i.e., ignoring the original primordial intelligence and space from which we emanated. This was followed by the birth of the inevitable ego. The ego now felt that it was a separate entity and *"There is a sense of seeing oneself as an external object, which leads to the first notion of 'other.' One is beginning to have a relationship with a so-called 'external' world."* Then the Tibetan master explains that, having become separate individuals, we then reacted to our projections rather than just seeing the world as it truly is (i.e., openness and intelligence.)

ACIM states that we have forgotten our true origin, which is what Chögyam Trungpa implied. He then explains that we set up a defence mechanism to protect our ignorance and so feelings come into being, then perceptions and then

---

[30] Chögyam Trungpa, *Cutting Through Spiritual Materialism*, p. 123, © 1973 by Chögyam Trungpa Reprinted by arrangement with Shambhala Publications Inc., Boston, MA, www.shambhala.com.

[31] Ibid., p. 124.

concepts. The last stage involves the creation of consciousness[32] and now the ego is completely developed.

The Tibetan master, Trungpa makes it clear that the ego, now well established, firmly believes in the world of solidity that has sprung into existence. *"From his* (i.e., the ego's) *confused point of view even thought becomes very solid and tangible…As far as he is concerned, form exists as solid and heavy form… He is too busy continuously trying to reinforce his own existence."* [33]

A parallel can be made with *ACIM*, which teaches that consciousness was created by the split mind: *"Consciousness, the level of perception, was the first split introduced into the mind after the separation, making the mind a perceiver rather than a creator. Consciousness is correctly identified as the domain of the ego. The ego is a wrong-minded attempt to perceive yourself as you wish to be, rather than as you are."* [34]

The *Course* also states, as does Chögyam Trungpa, that not only is the ego confused, but that practically everything we do in this world is done to reinforce the ego and its projections. *"The ego's goal is quite explicitly ego autonomy. From the beginning, then, its purpose is to be separate, sufficient unto itself and independent of any power except its own. This is why it is the symbol of separation…The ego is totally confused about reality, but it does not lose sight of its goal…"* [35] And earlier on in the Text, we are told that the ego developed "appetites" as a means of reinforcing its own existence. *"Appetites are 'getting' mechanisms, representing the ego's need to confirm itself. This is as true of body appetites as it is of the so-called 'higher ego needs.' Body appetites are not physical in origin. The ego regards the body as its home, and tries to satisfy itself through the body. But the idea that this is possible is a decision of the mind, which has become completely confused about what is really possible."* [36]

In short, we are stuck with a deluded ego, which is out to get as much of everything as it possibly can, and which has the aim of keeping us immersed in

---

[32] Consciousness is the last of the Five Skhandas or Five Heaps or Five Aggregates that one comes across quite frequently in Buddhist texts, i.e., form, feeling, perception, mental formations and consciousness.

[33] Ibid., p. 148 .

[34] *ACIM*, T42.

[35] *ACIM*, T203 & 204.

[36] *ACIM*, T58.

its illusory world of form because if we awoke to the Truth, that would mean its demise. Oh dear!

Bodhidharma was a fifth-century Indian Buddhist monk who introduced Zen to China. He gave many sermons, some of which have been translated into English by an American with the evocative pen name of Red Pine. Here is an excerpt from the Wake-up Sermon that particularly interests me. *"Mortals create delusions. And by using the mind to give birth to mind they always find themselves in hell."* [37] Here again we can see a comparison to the "split mind" of *ACIM*. God created Christ as part of his Mind. Christ then created extensions of the One Mind and then the "split" occurred and part of the mind decided to move away from its Source, fragment into pieces and create the world of form (*"using the mind to give birth to mind".*) At this point the ego came into being and with it came duality and multiplicity. The result is the world we see around us, and wouldn't you agree that many things on earth are indeed "hell" as the Bodhidharma stated? You only have to pick up a newspaper to find that out.

The Bodhidharma then said that, after having used the mind (the One Mind) to create the mind (ego) our state of mind is *"disturbed"* and, *"You go from one hell to the next. When a thought arises, there's good karma and bad karma, heaven and hell. When no thought arises, there's no good karma or bad karma, no heaven or hell."* Regarding the existence of the physical body, he has this to say: *"The body neither exists nor doesn't exist. Hence existence as a mortal and non-existence as a sage are conceptions with which the sage has nothing to do. His heart is empty and spacious as the sky."*

The *Song of Enlightenment* is an uplifting sermon that was written by an ancient Buddha called Ch'an Master Hsuan Chuen of Yung Chia. Here are a couple of verses that I found very relevant to the topic of illusion:

> *When one who is awakened to the Dharma-body [38], there are no*
> *objects;*
> *The essence of all things comes from the self-nature–Buddha!*
> *The Five Aggregates–mere floating clouds aimlessly coming and*

---

[37] Red Pine, *The Zen Teaching of Bodhidharma*, p. 61, North Point Press, New York, 1989.

[38] Dharma-body = one's True Nature, Self Nature or Original Nature , i.e., before the separation.

Going;
The Three Poisons [39]*–bubbles that appear and disappear.*

When Reality is attained, there is neither ego nor object,
And within that instant, the karma of eternal suffering is wiped
away.
If this is a lie to deceive living beings,
For ages as numberless as dust, let my own tongue be plucked
out....[40]

And I would like to quote one more verse, verse 43, of this lovely song, which is self-explanatory:

The Mind is a sensory organ ... things are its objects.
This duality is like dust on the mirror.
Wipe away the dust and the mirror shines brightly.
Mind and object vanish when the Self Nature is understood.

The *Eight Similes of Illusion* was written by Longchempa (1308–1364), an ancient Dzogchen [41] Master of the Nyingma [42] Buddhist tradition. I found the similes to be very relevant to this study on illusion:

1. *Dream: like a dream, objects perceived with the five senses are not there, but they appear through delusion.*

2. *Magical illusion: like a magic illusion, things are made to appear due to the temporary coming together of causes and conditions.*

3. *Hallucination or trompe-l'oeil: like a hallucination, things appear, yet there is nothing there.*

4. *Mirage: like a mirage, things appear, but they are not real.*

---

[39] The Three Poisons are greed, anger and ignorance.
[40] Ch'an Master Hsuan Chuen, *Song of Enlightenment,* Verses 2 & 3, online translation by Dragon Flower Ch'an Temple, www.dragonflower.org/song.html.
[41] According to the teachings of Dzogchen or Great Perfection our ultimate nature is pure, all-encompassing, primordial awareness that has no form of its own.
[42] The Nyingma School is one of the oldest schools of Tibetan Buddhism .

5.   *Echo: like an echo, things can be perceived, but there is nothing there, either inside or outside.*

6.   *City of gandharvas* [43]: *like a city of gandharvas, there is neither a dwelling nor anyone to dwell.* [44]

I don't think that leaves much room for doubt about the illusory nature of the world of phenomena. These similes refer to *dreams, hallucination* and *illusion,* words that can be found countless times in *ACIM.*

Huang Po was a Zen master who lived around 800 AD. His teachings took the form of parables that were presented as dialogues and anecdotes, and he dealt at length with the topic of illusion. I would like to make a couple of relevant quotes.

When asked whether the Buddha really liberates sentient beings, he replied: *"There are in reality no sentient beings to be delivered by the Tathagata* [45]*…Anything possessing ANY sign is illusory."* [46] Huang Po warned against using the conceptual mind to try to achieve enlightenment and further on in the same book, *The Zen Teaching of Huang Po,* he reiterated, *"Finally, remember that from first to last not even the smallest grain of anything perceptible has ever existed or ever will exist."*

According to most Buddhists, *cause and effect* produced the world of form and the ego. There is no personal God, no spirit, and no soul. But some Buddhists believe that all that exists is the One Mind. It is the one, all pervasive, limitless aspect of all that exists. Nothing else exists other than the one Mind. Huang Po spelt this out in no uncertain terms, *"Outside Mind, there is nothing. The green hills which everywhere meet your gaze and that void sky that you see glistening above the earth–not a hairsbreadth of any of them exists outside the concepts you have formed for yourself!"* [47]

---

[43] A low-ranking deva or nature spirit.

[44] www.rigpawiki.org/index.php?title=Eight_similes_of_illusoriness.

[45] The Buddha.

[46] John Blofeld, *The Zen Teaching of Huang Po,* pp. 70-71, © 1958 by John Blofeld. Used by permission of Grove/Atlantic, Inc. & by the Society of Authors on behalf of the Buddhist Society, www.societyofauthors.org.

[47] Ibid., p. 82.

I think a key word above is "concepts." Because if you look around you *do* see things; if you have a headache you *do* feel it; if you put the coffee filter machine on you *do* smell that wonderful aroma. But these things that we perceive with our senses are just concepts the ego has created to keep us welded to the physical world that it created. *"I have invented the world I see."* [48]

The same goes for emotions. We feel fear, anger, envy, humiliation, etc. and also empathy, happiness, attraction, love, etc. But these again have been created by the ego. The reason why we *all* experience them in the same way is because we are all joined together, having emanated from the same Source.

In our original state of perfection I don't think we would *feel* anything. As the *Course* states: *"Heaven is neither a place nor a condition. It is merely an awareness of perfect Oneness, and the knowledge that there is nothing else; nothing outside this Oneness, and nothing else within."* [49] There are no concepts of anything in Heaven. There is only God. There is only One of us all.

The concepts mentioned above in Huang Po's teaching can be equated with the term *idols* in *ACIM*. Both concepts of things in the world of phenomena and the concept of "me" or "mine" are illusory. *"A concept of the self is made by you. It bears no likeness to yourself at all. It is an idol, made to take the place of your reality as Son of God…Concepts are learned. They are not natural…Not one of them is true, and many come from feverish imaginations, hot with hatred and distortions born from fear…What is a concept but a thought to which its maker gives a meaning of his own? Concepts maintain the world. But they cannot be used to demonstrate the world is real…"* [50]

In fact, "idol" is anything created by the ego or desired by the ego or experienced by the ego and the *Course* frequently warns us that we should not seek to achieve happiness by anything outside ourselves. We cannot achieve lasting happiness by anything that was created by the ego. Therefore, sensual or material pleasures are all "idols" that will not lead us down the Path to God. *"Seek not outside yourself. For all your pain comes simply from a futile search for what*

---

[48] *ACIM*, W49, Lesson 32.
[49] *ACIM*, T384.
[50] *ACIM*, T656 & 657.

you want, insisting where it must be found. What if it is not there? Do you prefer that you be right or happy? Be you glad that you are told where happiness abides, and seek no longer elsewhere. You will fail. But it is given you to know the truth, and not to seek for it outside yourself." [51]

The fact that we are here experiencing life on this illusory planet indicates to us that we have been searching for happiness in the wrong places. We have been caught up in the concepts, idols and illusions of an illusory ego. *"No one who comes here but must still have hope, some lingering illusion, or some dream that there is something outside of himself that will bring happiness and peace to him. If everything is in him this cannot be so... The lingering illusion will impel him to seek out a thousand idols, and to seek beyond them for a thousand more. And each will fail him, all excepting one; for he will die, and does not understand the idol that he seeks is but his death...Whenever you attempt to reach a goal in which the body's betterment is cast as major beneficiary, you try to bring about your death. For you believe that you can suffer lack, and lack is death...All idols of this world were made to keep the truth within from being known to you, and to maintain allegiance to the dream that you must find what is outside yourself to be complete and happy. It is vain to worship idols in the hope of peace."* [52]

Back to Buddhism, I came across an interesting discussion about Zen Buddhism on the Internet. I found the following passage interesting because it deals with the notion of the unreality of the ego/human self. *"...the human self is built from social conventions, personal feelings and history and is, in this temporal sense, an illusion. This illusion of the self stands as a barrier between the true Self and a perception of reality. One only has to think of the false ideals like materialism and envy, etc., which absorb us in our daily lives, to understand the validity of the Zen perception of no–self.... After fully understanding the illusion of the self, the journey into Zen begins."* [53]

The *Lankavatara Sutra* is a Mahayana [54] text that is considered to be the words

---

[51] *ACIM*, T617.

[52] *ACIM*, T617 & 618.

[53] www.essortment.com/all/introductionzen_riej.htm.

[54] Mahayana is one of the three major schools of Buddhism, the other two being Theravada and Vajrayana.

of Buddha himself. It deals with the concepts of the One Mind, consciousness and the nature of reality. In Chapter 3 of the sutra we read, *"When it is recognised that the world as it presents itself is no more than a manifestation of mind, then birth is seen as no-birth and all existing objects, concerning which discrimination asserts that they are and are not, are non-existent and, therefore, un-born; being devoid of agent and action, things are un-born. If things are not born of being and non-being, but are simply manifestations of mind itself, they have no reality, no self-nature...."* [55] Here again we come across the idea of the mind creating the physical world and yet again the world of the ego is deemed to be an illusion because it has "no reality."

For an absorbing discussion about the belief systems of East and West, I would recommend the book, *"The Monk and The Philosopher"*, by Matthieu Ricard, a Buddhist monk and his father, Jean-Francoise Revel, a French philosopher. When asked by Revel about the nature of the "self," Ricard said that the attachment to the notion of the ego or self was an expression of ignorance and the cause of negative emotions. *"The very root of all negative emotions is the perceptions we have of ourselves as a person, as an 'I' that is an entity existing in itself, autonomously, either in the stream of our thoughts, or in our bodies. But if this self really exists, where is it? In our bodies? In our hearts? In our brains? Could it be spread out over the whole body? It's not difficult to see that the self doesn't exist anywhere in the body."* [56] Jean-Francois Revel pointed out to him that consciousness or awareness of one's self can exist without being located in any part of the body. His son replied that if one then tries to determine where the self is, such as in one's stream of consciousness, it cannot be in the past, which is dead, or in the future, which hasn't arrived yet, so it could only exist in the present. However, if this is the case, what are the characteristics of the self? He continued, *"The more you look for it, the less you can find anything. So finally the self seems to be no more than a label attached to an apparent continuity....To discover as a direct experience, through analysis and especially through contemplation, that the self has no true existence is a highly*

---

[55] *Lankavatara Sutra*, Chapter III, (based on Professor Suzuki's translation) www.sacred-texts.com/bud/bb/bb10.htm.

[56] Jean-François Revel & Mathieu Ricard, *The Monk and The Philosopher*, pp. 26-27, Thorsons, HarperCollins Publishers Ltd, London, Random House, Inc., NY, © 1998 by Jean-François Revel & Mathieu Ricard.

liberating process."

One of the books I couldn't put down recently was *Fingers Pointing Towards the Moon*, written by an Irish sage who went by the rather unusual name of Wei Wu Wei.[57] He gives an excellent summary of the relationship between reality and manifestation, i.e., the world of appearances, *"Reality is the Tao, the Absolute, other than which nothing is, immobile, timeless, space less... But Reality, being everything, is necessarily immanent, transcendent, subjacent, infused in everything that we can know, think, or imagine... Thus everything from a mirage to a mountain is unreal, yet everything from a mirage to a mountain must be a reflection of Reality."* [58]

I like the term "reflection of Reality" as it helps explain why it is we "see" or "perceive" the world of form that is all around us. It really isn't here but is simply a dim reflection of Heaven. It's like a mirage that appears real but when you get to it, there's nothing there. When we finally make it to Heaven, this world, or its reflection, will not be there any more either.

The *Diamond Sutra* and the *Heart Sutra* are perhaps two of the most famous Buddhist holy texts that are recited daily in Buddhist monasteries. The *Heart Sutra* (thought to have been written in the 1st Century AD) in particular deals with the concept of *sunyata* or emptiness, which is important to understand but it is quite a complicated concept. Edward Conze explains it very clearly in his book *Buddhist Wisdom—The Diamond Sutra and The Heart Sutra*. He says that sunyata deals with the concept, *"that something which looks like something much, is really nothing."* It is also a spiritual term that *"denotes the complete denial of, the complete liberation from, the world around us..."* And finally, as a technical term it denotes *"the absence of any kind of self."*[59]

Elaborating on the concept of emptiness on page 89, Edward Conze equates it with the "Beyond" and also with the "not-Beyond." *"The infinitely Far-away is not only near, but it is infinitely near. It is nowhere and nowhere it is not... Nirvana is the*

---

[57] Wei Wu Wei is a Taoist concept meaning effortless action.

[58] Wei Wu Wei, *Fingers Pointing towards the Moon*, p. 63, First Sentient Publications, Colorado, USA, 2003.

[59] Edward Conze, *Buddhist Wisdom—The Diamond Sutra and The Heart Sutra*, p. 85, Vintage Spiritual Classics, Vintage Books, Random House Inc. 2001.

same as the world. It is not only 'in' and 'with you', but you are nothing but it."

Again we can draw a parallel with the teachings of *ACIM* because, if we are Nirvana, then we must be divine ourselves. *"My mind is part of God's. I am very holy."* [60]

The doctrine of the "emptiness" of all things, or sunyata, was incorporated in the teachings of the Indian philosopher Nargajuna (around 150 AD), founder of the Madhyamaka (Middle Path) school of Mahayana Buddhism. He explained that all that exists is the "Absolute," which is devoid of any limitation. On an interesting website called "Believe", it is explained that, according to Nargajuna, the world of phenomena and experience are the products of thought forms that are imposed on the Absolute. *"These thought forms are the categories that reason creates in its attempt to apprehend the nature of reality. Since all phenomena in the world of experience depend upon these constructs of reason, they are purely relative and therefore ultimately unreal. The Absolute, on the other hand, is empty in the sense that it is totally devoid of artificial conceptual distinctions."* [61]

On the same religious information source website (which is a mine of information) it is also explained that, *"The Vijñanavada (consciousness doctrine) school of Mahayana ... taught that the mind alone exists and that the whole external world is an illusion projected by the mind. The dispelling of that illusion through meditation was presented as the path to enlightenment. In order to retain the basic assumption of Buddhism, the Vijñanavada School taught that after a full realization of the nature of all things, the mind dissolves in emptiness."*

ACIM also teaches that, at the very end, the world of phenomena will no longer exist and all that will remain will be God and His creations, i.e., all of us in spirit form but *without a physical form,* and we will be living eternally as part of the God and Christ. So although this differs somewhat from the Vijñanavada belief of the mind dissolving in emptiness, the lower self/part of the split mind/ego that perceives itself as an "individual" will no longer remain. *"When the thought of separation has been changed to one of true forgiveness, will the world be seen in quite another light; and one which leads to truth, where all the world must*

---

[60] *ACIM,* T53, Lesson 35.
[61] http://mb-soft.com/believe/txh/mahayana.htm .

disappear and all its errors vanish. Now its source has gone, and its effect are gone as well." [62]

On the University of Hong Kong's website the following explanation is given about the beliefs of Yogachara (which is another name for Vijñanavada) *"The elements of existence (Dharma) to which we cling when we have desires are the impermanent, unreal illusions generated by six or seven layers of consciousness. The cosmic sum of all consciousness was the Buddha-mind...The world of experience is a sequence of infinitesimal time-slices of consciousness.... That we desire the illusion to continue keeps the succession of conscious states alive and accounts for the continuity of objects and the coherence of objects of consciousness."* [63] So we see this is yet another belief system that states categorically that the world of appearance is just an illusion and it is our belief in it and our desire for the things of the world that keep the illusion alive.

On the same website we read, *"Our belief in the objects of consciousness are a kind of "clinging" that gives them permanence. If we can fully realize (real-ize or make real) or appreciate this illusory nature of the world, then it will cease. We will have escaped the grip of desire that stimulates consciousness and end any further illusions."* Thus, if we can become aware of the illusions created by the ego, we are more likely to overcome the ego. I will deal with this in greater depth in Chapter 8.

An interesting talk on the subject of emptiness was given a while ago at the Ch'an Meditation Center in New York, which is a branch of the Taiwanese Dharma Drum Mountain organisation. Entitled *Sun, Moon, Sky & Sea,* the talk was given by Master Jen-ch'un and focused on Mahayana beliefs. Master Jen-ch'un stressed that despite our intelligence we are so focused on attachments to desires and material things in the world that this is a major impediment to enlightenment. *"We constantly think, 'I think this' and 'I'm doing that' But the concept 'I' is only the understanding of an ordinary person holding on to an illusion. An enlightened person sees that the idea of 'I' is just the product of cause and conditions*

---

[62] *ACIM,* W413.

[63] www.hku.hk/philodep/Courses/religion/Buddhism .

coming together: a phenomenon that appears and will later disappear." [64]

Speaking about the doctrine of emptiness Master Jen-ch'un said, *"Emptiness in Buddhadharma does not mean that nothing exists. The concept of emptiness points out that things exist only because of cause and conditions, and that they are not permanent, independent, or sovereign...."* So here we clearly see the cause and effect belief of Buddhism. But it is important to be aware of the doctrine of emptiness; otherwise we will cling onto things (desires and material objects) because we are not aware that they are ultimately unreal. When that happens we become trapped. *"When you have such attachments, your whole being is obstructed by them. It is like being tied up. You cannot move around. You are enclosed, enslaved, and in bondage. On the other hand, if you truly understand emptiness you will not be attached; and when you are not attached, you will not be obstructed. So it is possible for you to move and to emerge from bondage."* And emerging from bondage is what this whole struggle and constant searching is all about.

As I look back on my life, I can now recognise the truth in those words of wisdom. I flitted from man to man in search of happiness. I gave a great deal of my life to my job, which brought with it fame and glamour for a time. But with hindsight I can clearly see that I really was enslaved in a way—trapped in the world of illusion, thinking that lasting happiness was to be found in a relationship or a job or in family life. Yes, there was a lot of joy, but did any of it last for more than a moment? No. The birth of my son gave me great joy but he grew up and now leads his own life, as he rightly should. My job on television had to end because if there's one place where you cannot be seen to age, it's in the public eye. As for my men, ah, what I fool I was. The passion soon faded away and I never could find someone with whom I could gel at the mental and spiritual levels. And now I am really glad about that, because I am sure that, as far as I was concerned, a long-lasting, seemingly permanent relationship could have been a diversion from my Path back home. I am sure this is not necessarily the case for others, but I could have become too wrapped up in a happy relationship that I may not have been motivated to search for the truth.

---

[64] Talk by Master Jen ch'un at the Ch'an Meditation Center, Elmhurst, New York, on July 16, 1989, translated by Ming-yee Wang and edited by Linda Peer, www.dharmadrumretreat.org.

Fortunately, at the back of my mind throughout these past 25 years I have always known that something was amiss with life on our planet. That's why I began searching for meaning at quite a young age. I started my quest by reading travel books that took me to all corners of the globe. Then I moved on to the three traditional orthodox religions in search of something with which I could truly connect. But I didn't find it. Then I moved on to studying other religious and spiritual beliefs and became attracted to both Hinduism and Buddhism because, to me, their teachings seemed to make more sense and they were more appealing both to my logical mind and to my intuition. Finally, I was somehow led to *A Course in Miracles* and I just knew that this was the closest to the truth I could get, at this moment in time. (It is interesting to note that *ACIM* teacher, Kenneth Wapnick has stated that the teachings of *ACIM* are *not* the final word of God and will be followed later on by—to use a technological term—an update. However, for now, and for the next few hundred years, the *Course* will show the way to those who feel inclined to pursue that particular Path.)

To return to the *Heart Sutra*, mentioned earlier in this chapter, it ends in the following lines:

"Therefore, one should know that Perfect Understanding is a great mantra, is the highest mantra, is the unequalled mantra, the destroyer of all suffering, the incorruptible truth. This is the mantra: Gate, gate paragate parasamgate bodhi svaha." [65]

Thich Nhat Hanh, in his commentaries on *The Heart of Understanding*, explains the sanskrit mantra as follows, *"Gate means gone. Gone from suffering to the liberation of suffering...Gone from duality into non-duality. Paragate means gone all the way to the other shore...In Parasamgate, sam means everyone, ... the entire community of beings...Bodhi is the light inside, enlightenment, or awakening. You see it and the vision of reality liberates you. And svaha is a cry of joy or excitement."* The "other shore" refers to crossing over from this illusory world of phenomena to the ultimate reality or, in other words, achieving enlightenment.

There is something about that mantra that I find quite appealing and I

---

[65] Reprinted from *The Heart of Understanding: Commentaries on the Prajnaparamita Sutra*, p. 49, (1988) by Thich Nhat Hanh with permission of Parallax Press, Berkeley, California, www.parallax.org.

sometimes recite it to myself as I am going about my daily chores. As I do so, I imagine I am speaking to my ego and telling it, "Gone, gone, I've gone away from you!" However, I don't think I am reciting the mantra as I really should be because Thich Nhat Hanh explains that it is a very powerful mantra but should not be recited like, *"singing a song, or with our intellect alone. If you practice the meditation on emptiness, if you penetrate the nature of interbeing* (being interconnected) *with all your heart, your body, and your mind, you will realize a state that is quite concentrated. If you say the mantra then, with all your being, the mantra will have power and you will be able to have real communication, real communion with Avalokitesvara,[66] and you will be able to transform yourself in the direction of enlightenment."* [67]

The Dhammapada is a collection of verses from the Pali Canon (Theravada Buddhist scriptures) that gives advice on numerous topics, including old age, evil, punishment, happiness, the Self, the Way, etc. It does not deal very much with the issue of the unreality of the self or ego. However, in Chapter 13 entitled *The World*, we read, *"Look upon the world as a bubble, look upon it as a mirage: the king of death does not see him who thus looks down upon the world."* [68] I think this implies that those who are aware that the world of form is an illusion or a mirage are able to conquer it by awakening and becoming liberated. In this way they avoid death by no longer having to keep reincarnating into a physical body.

Further on in the same chapter in verse 171 we read, *"Come, look at this glittering world, like unto a royal chariot; the foolish are immersed in it, but the wise do not touch it."* Those who are at the mercy of the ego, the *"foolish,"* are attracted by the things of the world, but the wise are aware of its illusory nature and turn away from it. And in verse 174 we are cautioned, *"This world is dark, few only can see here; a few only go to heaven, like birds escaped from the net."* This implies that we are trapped in the world of appearances and cannot see the truth. Only a few can *"escape."* How true that is. How many millions of us remain ensnared by all that

---

[66] Avalokitesvara is the Bodhisattva or disciple seeking Enlightenment who is mentioned in the Heart Sutra.

[67] Ibid., p. 51.

[68] *Dhammapada – A Collection of Verses from the Pali Canon of Buddhism*, p. 41, Chapter 13, verse 170, translated by F Max Muller, Red & Black Publishers, Florida, 2008.

the world around us has to offer? And how many actually become enlightened and therefore free of karma and of the need to live out any more lifetimes in the world of appearance?

As just mentioned, Theravada [69] Buddhism bases its teachings on the Pali Canon or Tipitaka, which is among the oldest records of the teachings of the Buddha. It has been the predominant religion of Burma, Thailand, Cambodia and Sri Lanka for many centuries. It is interesting to note that Buddhism is divided into two main branches, Mahayana and Theravada. Theravada is the northern branch and Mahayana the southern branch, which is practised mainly in China, Vietnam, Korea, Nepal, Tibet and Japan. Theravada tends to focus on the individual's spiritual evolution whilst Mahayana stresses compassion and helping others. However, both branches have enlightenment as their goal.

I decided it was time for me to have some first-hand knowledge of Theravada Buddhism and so I paid a visit to the Sri Saddhatissa International Buddhist Centre in Kingsbury, North London. Ten monks, mainly from Sri Lanka, live there and provide teaching and guidance for the Theravada Buddhist community in London. Located on a main road, it was surprisingly peaceful and quiet inside, with an open courtyard in which a large statue of the Buddha looked down upon a small pond, embellished by a fountain and decorative plants.

I was fortunate enough to have a short interview with two monks, Reverend Galayaya Piyadassi, who has lived in London for twenty years, and Reverend H. Mahinda. Rev Mahinda explained to me that change is at the foundation of their beliefs and he referred to the quantum physicist Donald Glaser, who invented the Bubble Chamber to measure the rapidity of change within an atom. He discovered that a single atom changes extremely rapidly. *"Everything changes but people think everything stands still,"* he told me. I asked him about the ego and he replied, *"In Theravada Buddhism we don't believe in the ego and we don't believe in the mind. Mind is not substance. The Lord Buddha said that there are only two things: space and nirvana. All other things are conditioned things and came into being because of cause and effect."* Rev Piyadassi said that it is important to understand the concept

---

[69] *Theravada* means the Teachings of the Elders.

of anattaa or egolessness that was central to the teachings of the Buddha. The personality, ego or soul are not real independent entities and do not exist either within time or in eternity. Everything we see is simply the outcome of cause and effect.

To clarify this matter Rev Mahinda made a useful analogy. *"A flame exists while there is oil and a wick. But if the wick or oil run out the flame will go out too. Where did it go? You can't say where it went, here or there. But as long as there are causes (oil and wick) there will be effects (the flame.) In other words, as long as we desire things in the world of phenomena these things will persist and appear to be real to us."*

I continued with my questions and asked, *"But where did the body come from?"*

"By thinking, the body comes" was the reply Rev Mahinda gave me. I quickly switched in my mind to *ACIM* and remembered that it was, in fact, the split mind that brought the ego, body and universe into being.

"What about enlightenment?" I asked him. *"Could I, as a householder, become enlightened in this lifetime?"* He smiled and said, *"Yes, everybody can, provided you don't have any cravings. It is easier for us because we, as monks, have overcome the feeling of lust. This is more difficult for lay people. But any cravings will lead to rebirth."*

I persisted with my questions and asked a rather silly one. *"What about food? Can you enjoy food or a nice cup of tea?"*

"You can enjoy meals but you mustn't like them too much because if you like something too much, that is craving. It means you are attached to these things and that will lead to rebirth," said Rev Mahinda. (Oh dear, I thought, I really will have to stop looking forward to my freshly ground, filtered coffee in the mornings.) I told him I had a son, whom I loved a lot, and asked him if that could stand in the way of enlightenment. He explained that if I was too attached to him then, yes, I would have to be reborn!

"What is the most important thing the average person can do to achieve enlightenment?" was my last question to Rev Mahinda. *"Give up lust and any other cravings. You don't have to give up your job, your car or your money. The Lord Buddha did not say you have to give everything away. You can have everything but just give up the attachment. It is a matter of letting go,"* he replied. He also added that you must

be aware that everything changes, understand this and concentrate your mind on the true nature of the world.

I always think if there is just a single word or sentence that you can relate to, whether in a book or in a discussion with somebody, then that book or discussion has been worthwhile. When I heard the words *"letting go,"* I knew that the long, hot journey out on the tube to the Sri Saddhatissa International Buddhist Centre had been worthwhile. Whilst the whole conversation was useful, the last phrase was something I decided I had to start working on— letting go. Not giving up my job or ignoring my precious son or cat, but simply trying to become a little more detached at the mental level and to develop equanimity in the face of all circumstances. Whatever comes, whatever goes, if you are able to remain detached or to let go of the things you have in your life, then you are making spiritual progress.

Now it was time for me to discover more about Tibetan Buddhism. So I hopped on another tube that took me, this time, to South London and to the Jamyang Buddhist Centre in Kennington. I was fortunate enough to be able to interview the resident Tibetan spiritual teacher and monk, Geshe Tashi Tsering (GTT.) I asked him firstly how the world of form came into being, according to Buddhism.

GTT: Unlike other religious traditions, Buddhism has a unique view on how the universe came into being. Buddhism calls it "dependent arising" or "dependent origination." Buddhism doesn't believe there is a supreme eternal being that created the universe. The external universe, such as the planet where we live, or the internal beings, I mean all the different species such as plants and all other species, came into being through a process of many causes and conditions. They came about through a process of interaction.

RN: So did they start off in spirit?

GTT: No, no, there is no concept of spirits. For example, for material things, as in modern physics, there is some kind of theory about particles. Well, that is almost exactly the same concept as in Buddhism.

RN: So do Tibetan Buddhists believe in the One Mind, the Absolute or the Void?

GTT: No, the One Mind concept is not accepted in the entire Buddhist tradition. Because as soon as you say "One Mind," then behind that there is the concept of eternity and we don't believe in that. So when we talk about the mind or consciousness we are referring to particular beings, such as your consciousness or my consciousness.

RN: But I thought in some Buddhist traditions there was the concept of the One Mind?

GTT: No, there is the concept of what we call emptiness or voidness. Buddha taught about selflessness or anatma; in other words, it was a theory of non-substantiality. External objects, like this table and cup and internal things, like feelings and thoughts, they do not have any kind of concrete, eternal, unchangeable nature.

RN: So are you saying that they are, in a way, unreal?

GTT: They are unreal in the sense of how they appear to us. They appear to us as concrete and substantial, but if we analyse them closely they do not possess that kind of nature.

RN: So are you saying they do not exist?

GTT: No, that is the wrong term. They do not exist *as they appear to us*. If we look at fear or joy—when they occur in us they appear to be substantial or concrete feelings. But if we look at them closely they do not exist as they appear to us. But that doesn't mean they do not exist.

RN: So if there is no One Mind, no creator, what is enlightenment all about?

GTT: We don't need to talk about enlightenment really. The Buddhist concept of enlightenment is overcoming confusion and doubts, freeing our present mind from misunderstandings such as attachment, aversion and ignorance. Freeing our minds from these things is enlightenment. To become an enlightened being you don't need some kind of supernatural power. It is a process of transforming our minds into a knowing mind or an awakened mind.

RN: So it's not being attached to anything around us?

GTT: Yes, you could put it like that.

RN: So do you recognise, in Buddhism, that we have an ego that we have to overcome?

GTT: Oh yes, in Buddhism the ego can be viewed as self-centredness. That is what we have to transform so that we become more altruistic. It is a matter of transforming the very egoistic concept of "I," although there will always be the feeling that I am doing this or I am doing that.

RN: Do you think the process of enlightenment is difficult? I mean why are there so few enlightened beings on the planet?

GTT: I can't say if there are very few or very many enlightened people as it is a very individual experience. But, you are right; regarding well-known enlightened people, there are very few. But if we look at our own minds and thoughts we know how difficult it is to transform them or to train them to reduce attachment and aversion.

RN: So what is the most important thing you can do to become enlightened. Is it meditation?

GTT: Meditation is one of the tools but there are three tools in Buddhism: morality, concentration and meditation. Meditation is not the only tool.

RN: What does concentration involve?

GTT: Concentration is a mental quality—the quality of clarity and stability of the mind—focusing the mind on one point or on one subject.

RN: Is it useful to study the scriptures and the sutras?

GTT: Yes, of course it is helpful because some of those scriptures and sutras are written by great teachers, teachers who themselves have gone through the process of training their minds and they have written down these texts, not like in modern times to becomes best-sellers, but to share their experiences with their fellow people.

RN: In some monasteries some of the sutras are recited every day. In what way is this beneficial?

GTT: One of the purposes of reciting sutras is to remind oneself how to conduct one's own daily life according to the spiritual path.

RN: What are the main features of Tibetan Buddhism and how does it differ from the other schools of Buddhism?

GTT: Tibetan Buddhism strongly follows the Mahayana Buddhist tradition so therefore, it has different practices and theories from Theravada Buddhism. Also Tibetan Buddhism has a Vijñanavada practice, which is an advanced practice that involves a lot of visualisations, such as visualising Buddha or other deities, such as the deity of compassion.

RN: From what I understand, Theravada Buddhism is more concerned with personal spiritual enlightenment whilst Mahayana Buddhism is more involved with service to humanity. Is this distinction correct?

GTT: Generally speaking, when Buddha taught His teachings, although it is difficult to establish historically, there were two groups of disciples, one concerned with self liberation and the other concerned not just with self liberation, but also with helping others. But both traditions practice compassion and altruism. Theravada Buddhists are not just concerned with self liberation.

RN: Does the rational mind or the intellect have any use in the process of enlightenment?

GTT: Yes, of course, because one of the main elements in becoming enlightened is dealing with ignorance and with misconceptions. So to deal with ignorance we need wisdom and to cultivate wisdom we need the intellectual process—thinking and analysing. That will reveal the truth and clear away the misconceptions.

RN: What can you tell me about the concept of emptiness or sunyata?

GTT: Emptiness is a concept that Buddha and other Buddhist teachers taught. Things are not intrinsically existent.

RN: Are you saying that it is all like an illusion?

GTT: Things are like an illusion but they are not illusions. For example, if you look in the mirror, you will see your face but within the mirror your face is not there. Therefore, through the process of looking at the mirror, our face appears to us in the mirror. Similarly all things and events appear to us to have a concrete, intrinsic nature, but if we search for the core nature of things within themselves, there is nothing.

RN: If we look at permanence, does anything last at all? Does consciousness last?

GTT: No, nothing lasts forever.

RN: I still don't quite understand the Buddhist concept of creation. You can't say there is a Void initially or an Absolute?

GTT: No, nothing.

RN: Do you believe that if someone carries out spiritual practices and meditates and so on, then he will have a better life in his next incarnation?

GTT: That is the hope, but the ultimate hope is for our mind to be free from attachment, aversion and ignorance.

RN: What part of me will come back in my next incarnation, if I don't have a soul?

GTT: Your sense of "I", of "me." Not the personality just your sense of identity.

RN: Is it like consciousness?

GTT: No, your sense of "I" only.

RN: But didn't you say we have to overcome the sense of "I"?

GTT: No, I said we have to overcome the *egoistic* sense of "I." There's a big difference.

RN: So if I overcome attachment, aversion and ignorance, can I achieve nirvana?

GTT: Nirvana is not something to be achieved. It is a process of overcoming attachment, aversion and ignorance. When these things no longer exist, then that is nirvana.

RN: What about time and space? Do they really exist?

GTT: In ultimate reality there is no time and no space. But relatively they do exist. Therefore when we say reality we need to clarify—is it relative truth or is it ultimate truth. In ultimate truth we can say there is no time or space.

And with that we came to the end of the discussion. It was a most interesting half hour and I was really grateful to Geshe Tashi Tsering for granting me the interview. Yet I must admit, as I walked back towards the Underground Station on my way home, I found it difficult to get my ahead around Buddhist cosmology and the Buddhist concept of cause and effect being the main factor in the creation of the universe. Some of it I could follow, but the *cause and effect* bit was still not that clear to me, especially as some of the Buddhist teachings I had researched did acknowledge the existence, not of a creator, but of a concept that could be termed the One Mind. Yet it has now become abundantly clear to me that, according to Buddhism, there definitely is no God, no spirit and no soul.

I decided to investigate further. Who better to turn to than His Holiness the Dalai Lama? I remember in one of his talks he had said that the interrelations of the natural laws of cause and effect were responsible for the emergence of the cosmos. But I needed to dig deeper.

In his book, *The Spirit of Peace*, His Holiness the Dalai Lama explained, *"Our scriptures assert that subtle particles existed in space before the creation of the universe. And they are still there.... We believe that any single universe can exist and then disintegrate, and immense cycles of time can elapse in the process. But the universe as a whole—the universal "spirit"—is always there. One might even imagine that this subtle spirit, which has incomparable power, is the primary principle of creation. Maybe at some point certain beings were delighted by the existence of this universe and that is why it exists."* [70]

On page 142 of the same book the Dalai Lama denied that this universe was created by God and explained that, *"...there are an infinite number of living beings whose karmic potential has collectively created the whole of this universe, as a fitting environment. The universe in which we live is created by our own aspirations and actions."* And he went on to explain that everything in the universe is interdependent and nothing exists on its own. The world is part of a stream of interrelated events that produces the appearance of things, their existence for a while and then their disappearance. I think he was referring here to the concept of dependent arising, which was mentioned during the interview with Geshe Tashi Tsering. According to the theory of dependent arising, or dependent origination, everything is interdependent and therefore phenomena arise only in dependence upon other causes and conditions.

The Dalai Lama also said that the world of phenomena is not as it appears to be. *"For instance, conventionally there is an 'I' undergoing pleasure and pain, accumulating karma and so forth, but when we search for this 'I' through analysis, we cannot find it. There is no whole which is separate from its parts. Thus phenomena are said to be illusions."* [71]

It is clear that there are major differences between the teachings of *ACIM* and Buddhism and yet there *are* some similarities. According to *ACIM* there definitely is a creator—God—but he did *not* create this universe or anything in it. He created only spirit and his creations have the same characteristics and qualities as He has. Thus they are eternal, changeless, infinite and perfect and they are all united with Him. That's why He could not have possibly created the universe and that's why physical phenomena are deemed to be an illusion. And here we see His Holiness the Dalai Lama saying something rather similar, i.e., *"phenomena are said to be illusions."*

I think that it is the emphasis above all on wisdom, compassion, karma,

---

[70] His Holiness the Dalai Lama with Frederique Hatier, *The Spirit of Peace – Teachings on Love, Compassion and Everyday Life,* p. 145, translated by Dominique Side, Thorsons, HarperCollins Publishers, London, 2002.

[71] Ibid., p. 142.

meditation and non-violence that attract me to Buddhism. It is not a religion that is based on dogma. It is a non-judgemental belief system that does not teach that those who follow different religions will all end up in hell, and Buddhist teachers and spiritual leaders do not force their beliefs upon others.

To return to the issue of the ego, Buddhist meditation master Sogyal Rinpoche speaks about the wisdom of egolessness in his book *The Tibetan Book of Living and Dying*. He points out that belief in the ego is the absence of true knowledge of who we really are and he warns about the deviousness of the ego. He explains that the ego is called *dak dzin* in Tibetan, which means *"grasping to a self,"* and he states, *"Ego is then defined as incessant movements of grasping at a delusory notion of 'I' and 'mine,' self and other, and all the concepts, ideas, desires, and activity that will sustain that false construction...So long as we haven't unmasked the ego, it continues to hoodwink us, like a sleazy politician endlessly parading bogus promises....Lifetimes of ignorance have brought us to identify the whole of our being with the ego....Yet ego is so convincing, and we have been its dupe for so long, that the thought that we might ever become egoless terrifies us...."* [72]

I can well imagine that the idea of being totally free of one's ego is terrifying because we have identified with it over aeons. It must be like giving up one's home and not having an alternative place of shelter. David Hawkins, that great enlightened author and teacher, described a moment or two of fear that he experienced during a mystical moment or *Samadhi* as he completely let go of the ego, *"Suddenly, without warning, a shift in awareness occurred and the Presence was there, unmistakable and all encompassing. There were a few moments of apprehension as the self died, and then the absoluteness of the Presence inspired a flash of awe."* [73] He then said the deep shock that he felt was compensated for by a feeling of love emanating from the Presence, yet there was more fear to come. *"There followed a moment of terror as the ego clung to its existence, fearing it would become nothingness. Instead, as it died, it was replaced by the Self as Everythingness...."* David Hawkins then described what it was like to be living in the world without an ego and it is

---

[72] Sogyal Rinpoche, *The Tibetan Book of Living and Dying*, pp. 116-117, © 1992, published by Rider. Reprinted by permission of The Random House Group Ltd & HarperCollins Publishers.

[73] David Hawkins, *Discovery of the Presence of God – Devotional Nonduality*, p. 293 & 295, Veritas Publishing, Arizona, 2006.

certainly very interesting reading. He explained that, *"to the ego, the fear of non-existence was formidable...."*

Yet if we look upon the ego as unreal, as something we have identified with in error, maybe when the happy moment of enlightenment arrives and we bid farewell to the ego forever, we won't be too terrified. Perhaps we could take heart from the following words of the Buddha, *"Never tire of reflecting on that which is yourself! Remember that the four elements composing your body, which are sometimes considered as real existences, are, in fact, all mere names, without personality, and that the so-called 'I' is but a passing guest, a thing of a moment; all things around us are only illusions!"* [74]

If all the things around us are only illusions, including the ego, then at the moment of liberation, when the time comes to surrender it completely, we are not really surrendering anything at all. So there should be no feeling of loss or fear. At that point we will simply be returning to our original state.

---

[74] *Sutra of Fort-Two Sections, Verse* 19, Journal of the Royal Asiatic Society, [Old Series, Volume XIX] [London, Harrison and Sons], [1862], {Scanned and edited by Christopher M. Weimer, March 2002} www.sacred-texts.com/journals/jras/os19-14.htm.

Chapter 3

Hinduism—Illusion

"The immortal cannot become mortal, nor can the mortal become immortal. For it is never possible for a thing to change its nature.... How can one who believes that an entity by nature immortal becomes mortal, maintain that the immortal, after passing through change, retains its changeless nature? .... No jiva (individual being) ever comes into existence. There exists no cause that can produce it. The supreme truth is that nothing is ever born." [75]

Although the concept of illusion or *maya* is at the foundation of the teachings of Hinduism, the world is not seen to be quite as "unreal" as it is in *ACIM*. Furthermore, according to some Hinduism teachings, God is believed to have played a part in the creation of the world of maya. So we read in *Shakti*, *"God says that on one side is his Maya (illusion), which keeps all the individual lives bound to this world, to this materialistic life, and on the other side is his bhakti, the devotion that grants liberation. They both belong to him."* [76]

---

[75] *Mandukya Upanishad*, Chapter 3, Verses 21, 22 & 48, e-book—English translation of Mandukya Upanishad by Swami Nikhilananda, www.naiveinspirations.com/?page_id=11.

[76] Shri Dhyanyogi Madjusudsandasji, *Shakti, An Introduction to Kundalini Maha Yoga*, p. 38, Dhyanyoga Centers, Inc., 2000.

This conflicts with the teachings of *ACIM*, which state categorically that the illusory world of the ego has nothing at all to do with God and, in fact, He is unaware that it even exists. However, the Holy Spirit, which is the *Voice for God*, has remained with us since the moment that the split mind veered off course and created the world of phenomena.

Yet we also read in the book *Shakti* on page 119 that, *"The main thrust of the process of the awakening of the Kundalini is the realization of the true nature of the Self, the ultimate union of jiva and God that brings a complete and permanent end to the suffering of the limited and Maya-bound form of existence."* So the world of illusion is seen to be both limited and the cause of suffering, just as it is in *ACIM*. According to the author of that book, sadhana or spiritual practice is the way that leads us out of the world of maya. *"The jiva is part of God but once separated, like the individual rays separate from the Sun, it forgets, becomes ignorant and entangled in Maya. The jiva is dependent on Maya, not independent like God. It goes through these fluctuations as long as it is unrealized, but once it realizes its identity it becomes stable and merges with God. That is why you have to do sadhana to reach God."* [77]

We can see from this passage that the jiva, which is the individual being or ego, is deemed to be as *"ignorant and entangled"* in the world of illusion as it is in *ACIM*. Also, the view that the ego has *forgotten* its true origins, i.e., that it was once a part of God, is similar to the teachings of *ACIM*. In fact, not only have we forgotten our divine origins but we are also dreaming. This is because the actual physical world in which we are living is as real as the world of dreams that we visit at night in our sleep. *"You are at home in God, dreaming of exile but perfectly capable of awakening to reality."* Furthermore, the ego made a conscious decision to forget that it is still at home in God and this decision has caused it to experience fear, which is at the root cause of all its actions. *"You are fearful because you have forgotten. And you have replaced your knowledge by an awareness of dreams because you are afraid of your dissociation, not of what you have dissociated."* [78]

In other words, we have forgotten that we are still as God created us and this

---

[77] Shri Dhyanyogi Madjusudandasji, *Shakti, An Introduction to Kundalini Maha Yoga*, p. 105, Dhyanyoga Centers, Inc., 2000.

[78] *ACIM*, T182 & 183.

engenders fear in our minds because at some, perhaps subconscious, level we do remember our true origins. We thus feel fearful and guilty for having "deserted" God and we believe He is wrathful and will punish us for the separation. Further on in the same section of the *Course* we read, *"Give up gladly everything that would stand in the way of your remembering, for God is in your memory. His Voice will tell you that you are part of Him when you are willing to remember Him and know your own reality again."* I think the last few words of this sentence are really what Buddhism, Hinduism and the mystical branches of other religions are concerned with, i.e., becoming aware of our true reality. In the terminology of *ACIM* this could be stated as follows: the whole point of learning about the false dreamlike world of the ego is to awaken from that dream and recognise that we are where we have always been — at home with God.

I think it is fairly obvious that *God is in our memory* because that would explain why millions of people around the world are searching and trying their utmost to find a path that will lead them Home. At some level, however enjoyable life is in this material world of ours, there is something that is missing. I think it is our memory or subconscious memory of God — of once having been at one with Him. I realise that there may also be millions of people who just don't believe in anything other than the material world, but I feel sure that it is just a matter of time before they change their minds. In their next or in a future lifetime they too will search for God and for eternal life. If there is one thing that this world of ours cannot possibly ever offer us, it is eternity. Everything is doomed to come to an end sooner or later and so the only option we really have is to choose eternity. If we don't choose it now, we will in a future lifetime. *"Here, with the journey's end before you, you see its purpose. And it is here you choose whether to look upon it or wander on, only to return and make the choice again."* [79]

So the *Course* is telling us that we can delay our return home but we can't put it off indefinitely and that one day we will choose the "journey's end." It stresses, *"The acceptance of the Atonement by everyone is only a matter of time. This may appear to contradict free will because of the inevitability of the final decision, but this is not so. You can temporize and you are capable of enormous procrastination, but*

---

[79] *ACIM*, T422.

*you cannot depart entirely from your Creator, Who set the limits on your ability to miscreate. An imprisoned will engenders a situation which, in the extreme, becomes altogether intolerable. Tolerance for pain may be high, but it is not without limit. Eventually everyone begins to recognize, however dimly, that there **must** be a better way. As this recognition becomes more firmly established, it becomes a turning point. This ultimately reawakens spiritual vision, simultaneously weakening the investment in physical sight."* [80]

Looking around me I see so much beauty. I love the forests, the flowers, the wildlife, the mountains, the rivers and the oceans. But there is still something about it all that doesn't quite ring true, at least in my opinion. Maybe it has something to do with our consciousness of the transiency not only of human existence, but of everything around us. With its usual clear-cut logic the *Course* states, *"The world as you perceive it cannot have been created by the Father, for the world is not as you see it. God created only the eternal and everything you see is perishable. Therefore, there must be another world that you do not see"* [81] And it is this other world that so many of us are determined to discover. Following the teachings of *ACIM* is one way of doing that.

A film that made a big impact on me several years ago was *The Truman Show* starring Jim Carey. In fact, I left the cinema feeling particularly uneasy. Readers may remember the fantasy movie, which was about an insurance salesman who was living a fake life. All the people in his life were actors playing their roles in a worldwide live TV show. All the places Truman went to on Seahaven Island were giant set pieces and he was unaware that everything he did was being filmed and aired on TV. But with time he gradually became suspicious as he found his life was just too repetitive and seemed to be as though it was in a loop. He decided to try to escape from it all but was unable to do so. Everyone conspired to thwart his plans and keep him trapped on the island. I found a scene near the end of the film to be very claustrophobic. Just as he thought he had managed to flee and was sailing away to freedom with a huge smile on his face, his boat bumped into a wall that had been done up to look as though it was

---

[80] *ACIM*, T21 & 22.
[81] *ACIM*, T210.

the open sky. He then finally discovered that everything all around him was, in fact, part of a huge TV studio. Truman, a very genuine man, had been living a phoney life.

Although the film was really about the extent of the intrusion of the media in our lives and about our addiction to television, I can definitely see a connection between *The Truman Show* and the world of the ego. Here we are living a fake life in an unreal world believing it to be real. There really is only one thing for us to do—escape! In fact, in the last scene of the film, the director of *The Truman Show* tries his best to convince Truman to remain in that safe and secure environment. But Truman had the guts to decide to walk away from it and make a new start in the "real" world. I believe that the ego would like us to remain in its grip forever and it tries to convince us that it can provide security and shelter for us. But can it? Isn't everything in the world we see really extremely fragile and unpredictable? The only true safety and shelter we will ever find will be when we return to our Source.

Something else that interested me in that film is a very relevant comment made by the director of the TV show. When asked why Truman had not realised that his world was not real, he replied, *"We accept the reality of the world with which we are presented."* Isn't that exactly what we are all doing right now? We see what is around us, we read the various scriptures and we believe what we see and what we read. But what if this world actually is unreal? What if all is *not* as it seems?

Speaking about the unreal world of the ego, *ACIM* tells us that we substituted fear for love and that was a serious error. *"You who believe God is fear made but one substitution. It has taken many forms, because it was the substitution of illusion for truth; of fragmentation for wholeness…You do not realize the magnitude of that one error. It was so vast and so completely incredible that from it a world of total unreality had to emerge…But nothing you have seen begins to show you the enormity of the original error, which seemed to cast you out of Heaven, to shatter knowledge into meaningless bits of disunited perceptions, and to force you to make further substitutions. That was the first projection of error outward. The world arose to hide it, and became the screen on which it was projected and drawn between you and the truth…Do you really think it strange that a world in which everything is backwards and upside down arose from this projection of error? It was inevitable."* [82] From this passage we can clearly see that the ego created a world of its own in which to escape from its original error (the separation from God) and this world is totally unreal, just as Truman's world was.

If we turn now to the philosophy of an enlightened Indian sage, Bhagavan Sri Ramana Maharishi (1879–1950), he explained that one should not think of one's body when one uses the word "I." The individual is the Self that dwells in the body, but it is the mind that has caused all the problems of misidentification: *"It is the Mind which relates the body with the Self. Mind, with all the thoughts, concepts, desires, hopes, etc., creates the false ego, a false phenomenon, in which the Mind in turn moves.... One's movements within the sphere of this false ego causes misery...."* [83] His teachings are quite similar to those of *ACIM* as he too emphasises that the ego has no real existence. Referring to the ego, further on in the same book, he said, *"Trying to trace it and find its source, one will realise that it has no separate or independent existence....When the real 'I' ceases to be known this erroneous 'I' comes in the front...."* And he added that the ego needs to have concepts, thoughts and memories to keep it going. However, one important difference between Maharishi's teachings and the *Course* is that the latter states that the soul or Self does *not* dwell in the body because there is no body.

Maharishi was asked by a disciple about pain in the world and pointed out that pain and hunger are very real experiences to us. He replied that when dreaming we feel pain and hunger but upon awakening they vanish. Similarly, *"...just as when you woke up from the sleep you realised that the pain in the dream was unreal, you will also realise when you become a Jnani, a man of wisdom, that even the hunger and the pain which you felt when you are in the wakeful state is also not real but the response of your mind to the stimuli of the senses of the gross body."* [84]

Maharishi referred there to a Jnani, an enlightened sage who has followed the path of jnana yoga or the yoga of knowledge. As the reader may be aware, there

---

[82] *ACIM*, T372 & 373.

[83] Nagesh D. Sonde, *Philosophy of Bhagavan Sri Ramana Maharishi*, p. 26, Sri Satguru Publications, Delhi, 2005.

[84] Ibid., p. 33.

are many branches of yoga, including bhakti yoga, which is the yoga of devotion; karma yoga, the yoga of service; hatha yoga, the yoga that involves the training and purification of the physical body; raja yoga, the yoga that focuses on meditation and the training of the mind; kriya yoga, which involves breathing techniques to promote spiritual development; and Kundalini yoga, which involves awakening the Kundalini energy that lies dormant in the base chakra. There could be other forms of yoga, but for the purposes of this study I would like to stress that it is jnana yoga, above all the others, that deals with the concept of the non-reality of the ego.

"…This is the basis of all ignorance that we, the immortal, the ever pure, the perfect Spirit, think that we are little minds, that we are little bodies; it is the mother of all selfishness. As soon as I think that I am a little body, I want to preserve it, to protect it, to keep it nice, at the expense of other bodies; then you and I become separate. As soon as the idea of separation comes, it opens the door to all mischief and leads to all misery." [85] This passage could well have been something we could have come across in *ACIM*. Actually it was written by an Indian sage, Swami Vivekananda (1863–1902), who lived over a hundred years ago and who introduced yoga and the Vedanta [86] to the West. He was an eminent disciple of Sri Ramakrishna and he dealt at length with the topic of illusion or maya in his lectures and discussions.

With reference to the non-existence of the physical world, he explained, *"It means that it* (the world) *has no absolute existence. It exists only in relation to my mind, to your mind, and to the mind of everyone else….; it has no unchangeable, immovable, infinite existence. Nor can it be called non-existence, seeing that it exists, and we have to work in and through it. It is a mixture of existence and non-existence."* [87] This may seem to differ somewhat from the teachings of *ACIM* but the *Course* does say that, although our world is unreal, it does appear to be real to those of us who are actually trapped in time and space and, therefore, it cannot be denied in that sense.

---

[85] Swami Vivekananda, *Jnana Yoga*, p. 40, Advaita Ashrama, Calcutta, 1993.

[86] Vedanta is the Hindu spiritual tradition that is concerned with understanding the ultimate nature of reality and thereby achieving enlightenment.

[87] Ibid., pp. 51-52.

On the topic of maya or illusion, Vivekananda explained that those of us trapped in the veil of illusion are forced to experience good and bad, happiness and sorrow, laughter and tears, etc., *"Both the forces of good and evil will keep our universe alive for us, until we awake from our dreams and give up this building of mud pies. That lesson we shall have to learn and it will take a long, long time to learn it."* [88] So he too refers to life on earth as a "dream." He points out that eventually we will tire of this world of illusions and, *"There comes a time when the mind awakens from this long and dreary dream—the child gives up its play and wants to go back to its mother."* Explaining that satisfying desires only stokes the fire and actually increases them, he said, *"This is true of all sense-enjoyments, of all intellectual enjoyments, and of all the enjoyments of which the human mind is capable. They are nothing; they are within Maya, within this network beyond which we cannot go."*

Vivekananda discusses another topic that *ACIM* also deals with, and that is how the ego, which is finite, can (or rather cannot) express God, Who is infinite. *"…philosophers naturally ask for a logical fundamental basis for the statement that the finite can fully express the Infinite. The Absolute and the Infinite can become this universe only by limitation. Everything must be limited that comes through the senses, or through the mind, or through the intellect; and for the limited to be the unlimited is simply absurd, and can never be. The Vedanta, on the other hand, says that it is true that the Absolute or the Infinite is trying to express itself in the finite, but there will come a time when it will find that it is impossible, and it will then have to beat a retreat, and this beating a retreat means renunciation which is the real beginning of religion."* [89]

Whilst ACIM does not say that the Infinite tries to express itself in the finite, the idea of limitation crops up several times. *"The body cannot know. And while you limit your awareness to its tiny senses, you will not see the grandeur that surrounds you. God cannot come into a body, nor can you join Him there. Limits on love will always seem to shut Him out, and keep you apart from Him. The body is a tiny fence around a little part of a glorious and complete idea. It draws a circle, infinitely small, around a very little segment of Heaven, splintered from the whole, proclaiming that within it is your kingdom, where God can enter not."* [90] So not only do we deny ourselves access

---

[88] Swami Vivekananda, *Jnana Yoga*, p. 63, Advaita Ashrama, Calcutta, 1993.
[89] Ibid., p. 64.
[90] *ACIM*, T390.

to the infinite but we also actually try to keep God out and continue in our finite state, set up by the ego.

Further on in the same section of *ACIM* we are called upon to broaden our horizons and expand our vision. Comparing the split mind/ego with a tiny sunbeam and a miniscule ripple on the surface of the ocean, we are told that the Self (the higher self or "right" part of the mind that has remained united with Christ and God) is unaware of the separate ego. *"Like to the sun and ocean your Self continues, unmindful that this tiny part regards itself as you. It is not missing; it could not exist if it were separate, nor would the whole be whole without it....This little aspect is no different from the whole, being continuous with it and at one with it. It leads no separate life, because its life is the oneness in which its being was created. Do not accept this little, fenced-off aspect as yourself. The sun and ocean are as nothing beside what you are. The sunbeam sparkles only in the sunlight, and the ripple dances as it rests upon the ocean. Yet in neither sun nor ocean is the power that rests in you...This little self is not your kingdom. Arched high above it and surrounding it with love is the glorious whole, which offers all its happiness and deep content to every part. The little aspect that you think you set apart is no exception."* [91]

I mentioned earlier in this chapter that Swami Vivekananda was a prominent disciple of Paramahamsa Sri Ramakrishna. Ramakrishna (1836-1886) is an unusual sage because he practised the Hindu religion as well as other religions and he came to the realisation that, although there are many religions, there is only one God. Like Vivekananda he also taught that maya or illusion was a major obstacle on the path of disciples. Speaking of the "evil of Maya" he said, *"Maya is nothing but the egotism of the embodied soul. This egotism has covered everything like a veil. All troubles come to an end when the ego dies. If by the grace of God a man but once realizes that he is not the doer, then he at once becomes a jivanmukta. Though living in the body, he is liberated. He has nothing else to fear."* [92]

However, Ramakrishna did not state that the ego was an illusion and he spoke about the individualised or embodied soul as being distinct from the

---

[91] *ACIM,* T391 & 392.

[92] R.R. Diwakar, *Paramahansa Sri Ramakrishna,* pp. 228-229, Bharatiya Vidya Bhavan, Mumbai 400 007 – 1980.

higher Self. *"There is the individualised self and there is the higher Self. Every individual is connected with the higher Self...The body is transient and unimportant. Why then is it so much looked after? The virtuous cannot but take care of the body, the temple of the soul in which God has manifested Himself, or which has been blessed by God's advent."* [93] So here we see a different opinion to that of *ACIM*, which does *not* consider the body to be the temple of the soul. And yet if we look at God-realisation, which Ramakrishna, like all sages, believed to be the ultimate goal, he said that the individual being upon enlightenment would become one with God.

This is the same view as *ACIM* that states that we are really one with God all along, but it just appears to us that we are living in our own world, the world of phenomena and of duality. *"We share one life because we have one Source, a Source from which perfection comes to us, remaining always in the holy minds which He created perfect. As we were, so are we now and will forever be. A sleeping mind must waken, as it sees its own perfection mirroring the Lord of life so perfectly it fades into what is reflected there. And now it is no more a mere reflection. It becomes the thing reflected, and the light which makes reflection possible. No vision now is needed. For the wakened mind is one that knows its Source, its Self, its Holiness."* [94] In other words, we were created perfect but at the time of the separation or the splitting of the mind we fell into a deep sleep. The life we are living in this world of duality is similar to a dream and when we awaken we will realise that we are one with God and always have been.

> *If a thing is non-existent both in the beginning and in the end, it is necessarily non-existent in the present. The objects that we see are really like illusions; still they are regarded as real.*[95]

---

[93] R.R. Diwakar, *Paramahansa Sri Ramakrishna*, pp. 222-224, Bharatiya Vidya Bhavan, Mumbai 400 007 – 1980.

[94] *ACIM*, W320.

[95] *The Mandukya Upanishad,* Chapter 2, verse 6, English translation by Swami Nikhilananda, www.naiveinspirations.com/?page_id=11 .

That passage is an extract from the Mandukya Upanishad, which is one of the shortest Upanishads, the scriptures of Hindu Vedanta. It deals with the mantra Aum and three states of waking, dreaming and sleeping, and the transcendent fourth state of enlightenment or illumination. I believe that the verse quoted above is talking about the world of form, i.e., the human body and all the objects in the manifested world. We were created as spirit not as bodies. Therefore, if our bodies (and the tangible objects in the world) were non-existent initially and they are non-existent in transcendental consciousness, when we move beyond the world of form, then they are not really existent in between the beginning and the end.

> *In dreams, what is imagined within the mind is illusory and what is cognized outside by the mind, real; but truly, both are known to be unreal. Similarly, in the waking state, what is imagined within by the mind is illusory and what is cognized outside by the mind, real; but both should be held, on rational grounds, to be unreal.*[96]

In these two verses we see that the waking state is compared to the sleeping state and all that the mind imagines and perceives is said to be unreal.

I think it is important to take a look at the following verses of the Mandukya Upanishad, which I quoted at the beginning of this chapter, because they deal with non-duality:

> *The unborn Atman* [97] *becomes manifold through maya and not otherwise. For if the manifold were real, then the immortal would become mortal.*

> *The disputants assert that the unborn entity (Atman) becomes born. Now can one expect that an entity that is birthless and immortal should become mortal?*

---

[96] *The Mandukya Upanishad,* Chapter 2, verses 9 & 10, *www.naiveinspirations.com/?page_id=11.*

[97] The Atman denotes the soul in Hinduism or one's true or higher Self. It is referred to as spirit in *ACIM,* which does not use the word "soul".

> *The immortal cannot become mortal, nor can the mortal become
> immortal. For it is never possible for a thing to change its
> nature.*
>
> *How can one who believes that an entity by nature immortal
> becomes mortal, maintain that the immortal, after passing
> through change, retains its changeless nature?*
>
> *Coming into birth may be real or illusory; both views are
> equally supported by the scriptures. But that view which is
> supported by the scriptures and corroborated by reason is alone
> to be accepted and not the other.*[98]

So here we see a clear attempt to determine whether or not the world of objects has any reality to it. In this Upanishad we are advised to use reason to reach the truth of the matter, as there are scriptures that support both views. However, I feel that, according to what is written here, the author of this scripture takes the view that the immortal *cannot* become mortal.

In verses 27 to 29 another comparison is made between the dream state and the waking state:

> *What is ever existent appears to pass into birth through maya,
> yet from the standpoint of Reality it does not do so. But he who
> thinks this passing into birth is real asserts, as a matter of fact,
> that what is born passes into birth again.*
>
> *The unreal cannot be born either really or through maya. For it
> is not possible for the son of a barren woman to be born either
> really or through maya.*
>
> *As in dreams the mind acts through maya, presenting the
> appearance of duality, so also in the waking state the mind acts
> through maya, presenting the appearance of duality.*

---

[98] *The Mandukya Upanishad*, Chapter 3, verses 19-23, www.naiveinspirations.com/?page_id=11.

And in the final verse of Chapter 3 a decision is reached:

No jiva (individual being) ever comes into existence. There exists
no cause that can produce it. The supreme truth is that nothing
ever is born.

I think that Upanishad is well worth reading and trying to understand even though some passages need to be read several times in order for their meaning to be clearly grasped.

I came across another account of the Hindu view of illusion on the Internet. The author, Octavian Sarbatoare, said that the concept of maya or illusion is a key component of the Upanishads (Hindu scriptures) and is seen to be the obstacle that stands in the way of knowledge of Brahman and enlightenment. *"Essentially, this illusion, Maya is described as a veil covering the access to the knowledge of the ultimate reality as Brahman. The realm of Maya containing both negative and positive kinds of actions (Karmas) like suffering, misery, joy, etc., is seen as a powerful illusion. Maya is thus believed to keep us trapped in the world of Samsara, the life of transmigrations in which there is a cyclical birth-death rotation over a considerable period of time."* [99] Once again maya is deemed to be like a veil that clouds reality. There is also a distinct similarity with the teachings of *ACIM* as it too points out both pleasure and pain are to be found in this world of illusion, but it stresses that ultimately the ego can only produce pain as everything in the world of phenomena is transient and ends in death. The *Course* also clearly points out that we *are* trapped if we believe in the ego. *"Would you be hostage to the ego or host to God? Let this question be asked you by the Holy Spirit every time you make a decision. For every decision you make does answer this, and invites sorrow or joy accordingly."* [100]

Octavian Sarbatoare continues, *"Maya, the illusion, appears thus to be a kind of mental prison in which most of the humanity is trapped, thus rendered unable to see the true reality of Brahman that is existent beyond the veil of the phenomenal world. The Upanishadic literature is consistent to affirm that only by removing the veil of ignorance, the human true nature can be accessed, so that Brahman be experienced at a personal*

---

[99] Octavian Sarbatoare *Tattvamasi ('that you are') in the Upanishads.*
   www.geocities.com/Athens/Olympus/3588/tattvam.htm .
[100] *ACIM,* T307.

level."

So it would seem that, although the Hindu view is that the mind has to be transcended if one is to experience illumination, there is still a place for study and logical thinking, at least in the initial stages of one's spiritual practice. We need to know about the nature of maya—about the devious tactics of the ego—if we are to ever stand a chance of releasing ourselves from its clutches. Study is needed in order to *"remove the veil of ignorance. "*

Indian author K. R. Paramahamsa, in his excellent book on Advaita Vedanta, gives a more complex description of maya *"... it is neither existent, nor non-existent, nor both. It is not existent, for the Brahman alone is the existent (sat [101].) It is not non-existent, for it is responsible for the appearance of the world. It cannot be both existent and non-existent as such a statement is self-contradictory. It is thus neither real, nor unreal; it is Mithya. But it is not a non-entity or a figment of imagination like the son of a barren woman.... When right knowledge dawns, the real nature of the world is realized as Maya disappears."* [102] Similarly, *ACIM* tells us that once we are able to overcome the ego and return to our Source, the world of illusions will simply disappear.

Paramahamsa goes on to explain on page 164 that the world of maya has a practical reality. *"The determinate world exists. But for a soul liberated, the determinate world gets transformed into the pure being of the Brahman...But the determinate world continues to exist for the un-liberated souls as empirically as ever. It is like 'It neither exists, nor does not exist, nor both, nor neither' and also 'It is neither true, nor false, nor both, nor neither.'"* That's quite a statement to try to understand!

Although *ACIM* dwells at great length upon the fact that the world of the ego is unreal as is the human body, it also states that we cannot completely *deny* its existence. *"...The body is merely part of your experience in the physical world. Its abilities can be and frequently are over-evaluated. However, it is almost impossible to deny its existence in this world. Those who do so are engaging in a particularly unworthy form of denial. The term 'unworthy' here implies only that it is not necessary to protect the mind by denying the unmindful. If one denies this unfortunate aspect of the*

---

[101] Sat = Reality.
[102] K. R. Paramahamsa, *Tat Sat*, p. 162, Total Recall Publications Inc. Texas, 2007.

mind's power (i.e., the creation of the physical body), *one is also denying the power itself."* [103] And we are told that whilst we believe we are in the body, the body does have a purpose. It is a *"learning device"* to be used to bring about the Atonement or change in perception, i.e., to lead us from illusion to truth. This is explained in the following manner: *"You can use your body best to help you enlarge your perception so you can achieve real vision, of which the physical eye is incapable. Learning to do this is the body's only true usefulness."* [104]

Paramahamsa's view of the creation of the body is comparable to that of *ACIM*. He states, *"It is the mind that creates the body by mere thoughts, just as the potter makes a pot out of clay. It creates new bodies and brings about the destruction of what exists, and all this is by mere wish.... It creates the appearance of the body within itself. But in ignorance, one sees the physical body in gross physical vision as different from and independent of the mind."* [105] And later on in his book he stresses that the world is simply a hallucination, and when hallucinations are experienced by many individuals they become accepted as reality.

The omnipresence of God is a prominent Hindu belief. *"God dwells in the heart of all beings Arjuna: thy God dwells in thy heart."* [106] Not only is the "divine spark" believed to exist in every human being, but also in all of God's creation. In fact, the Hindu greeting *namaste* means the *divine in me greets, or bows to, the divine in you.* I have always been drawn to this belief and frequently remember God as I listen to a wonderful piece of classical music, as I walk in a beautiful green forest or as I gaze across a magnificent landscape. But then I studied *ACIM*, which insists that everything in the world of phenomena is unreal, so I became rather confused. I therefore gave the matter some thought.

There are two ways of looking at it. I could see these things (the music, forest, landscape) as *symbols* of God and, therefore, even if He did not create them, I can use them to remember Him. Alternatively, I could look at it from the Hindu perspective. They believe, as I have just mentioned, that God is in everything—

---

[103] *ACIM*, T23 & 24.
[104] *ACIM*, T15.
[105] K. R. *Tat Sat*, pp. 15-16, Total Recall Publications Inc., Texas 2007.
[106] Juan Mascaro, *The Bhagavad Gita*, Chapter 18, verse 61, p. 120, Penguin Books, 1988.

the universe, humans, animals and plants. But they also believe that our true nature is spirit and only spirit is real. All the rest is *maya* or illusion. So I think we could interpret their belief as God is in *both the unreal and the real.* All is God, even the unreal world that we perceive with our senses.

"How holy is the smallest grain of sand, when it is recognized as being part of the completed picture of God's Son! The forms the broken pieces seem to take mean nothing. For the whole is in each one. And every aspect of the Son of God is just the same as every other part." [107] So this would seem to support the Hindu belief of everything around us being holy or divine. In Lessons 29 and 30 of *ACIM* it is explained exactly why this is the case. *"God is in everything I see"* and *"God is in everything I see because God is in my mind."* [108] A little further on in the Workbook, in Lesson 56 on page 93, a more detailed explanation is given. *"God is in everything I see. Behind every image I have made, the truth remains unchanged. Behind every veil I have drawn across the face of love, its light remains undimmed....God is still everywhere and in everything forever...In my own mind, behind all my insane thoughts of separation and attack, is the knowledge that all is one forever...."* And this corresponds closely with the Hindu view of God's omnipresence.

This view of God was expounded by the Indian sage and saint Swami Sivananda Saraswati (1887-1963.) He believed that everything in the world has the divine spark of God within it. God is everywhere and in everything. *"God dwells in all beings as life and consciousness. God is in the roar of a lion, the song of a bird, and the cry of a babe. Feel His presence everywhere...God, seen through the senses, is matter. God, seen through the intellect, is mind. God, seen through the spirit is Atman or the Self."* [109] And yet Swami Sivananda spoke at length about *maya*, which he described as the illusory power of God. He warned that *maya* keeps the individual trapped in the cycle of life, death and rebirth. On page 333 of the book *Bliss Divine,* he states, *"Maya is manifest in the human individual as mind. Mind alone is Maya. Maya is only mind. Control of mind is control of Maya...."* And he listed

---

[107] *ACIM,* T600.

[108] *ACIM,* W45 & 47.

[109] Swami Sivananda, *Bliss Divine – A Book of Spiritual Essays on the Lofty Purpose of Human Life and the Means to its Achievement,* pp. 190-191, compiled by Sri Ananthanarayanan, The Divine Life Society, Himalayas, India, 2006.

ways in which *maya* lures people away from reality: *"Smile, affection, comfort, name, fame, kind words, wife, children, house, property, respect, honour, power, prestige, position, titles, heaven are all Maya's tempting baits to ensnare the deluded souls. Beware of Maya's charms."* When described like this it is easy to see how *maya* and its devious methods can be compared to the ego that is spoken about in depth in *ACIM* and which I will deal with in greater detail in Chapter 7.

Swami Sivananda referred to *maya* as "the great illusion" and said, *"By the force of this Maya, the whole world appears in the place of the Supreme Being."* (In *ACIM* the ego is responsible for the appearance of the phenomenal world that also seems to take the place of God.) Swami Sivananda also said, *"Maya exists as the cause of perception of the manifoldness of the universe, but in truth, it has no reality. It is also an appearance like the appearances which it causes. It cannot be said to exist, nor can it be said not to exist. It is the false cause of the seeming appearances."* [110] I find these last few sentences to be really interesting. *Maya* causes the multiplicity that we see in the world of form, but it has no reality. *ACIM* says that at the time of the separation the ego produced the multiplicity of the phenomenal world but it has no reality.

I would like to make one final comparison between the teachings of the Indian sage and *ACIM*. Speaking of objects that we perceive, Swami Sivananda said, *"The perception of an object is unreal, because objects are creations of the mind. An object has got a particular form, because the mind believes it to be so. In fact, objects of both the dreaming and the waking states are unreal.... The unreal world appears as real, whereas it is in reality a long dream arisen in our mind. As in dream, so in the waking state, the objects seen are unsubstantial....This world is nothing but a long dream."* [111] In Lesson 1, in the Workbook of *ACIM* we are told, *"Nothing I see in this room (on this street, from this window, in this place) means anything"* and in Lesson 2, *"I have given everything I see in this room (on the street, from this window, in this place) all the meaning that it has for me."* This is identical to Swami Sivananda's view that objects are unreal or have no meaning and an object has a particular form

---

[110] Swami Sivananda, *Bliss Divine – A Book of Spiritual Essays on the Lofty Purpose of Human Life and the Means to its Achievement*, p. 330, compiled by Sri Ananthanarayanan, The Divine Life Society, Himalayas, India, 2006.

[111] Ibid., pp. 146-147.

because the mind believes it to be so.

Yet we saw earlier how *ACIM* teaches us that *"God is in everything I see"* (which is the same view as Swami Sivananda's) and also *"God is in everything I see because God is in my mind."* So how can all the objects one sees be meaningless and yet, at the same time, God is in everything one sees? This dichotomy is explained in *ACIM* like this: *"Certainly God is not in a table, for example, as you see it. Yet we emphasized yesterday that a table shares the purpose of the universe. And what shares the purpose of the universe shares the purpose of its Creator."* [112] I believe that the *Course* is talking about two different levels of "seeing." The first level involves the physical eyes of the illusory body, which are used to see objects that are not really there, but are seen because they have been created by the ego, which has given its own meaning to all that it created. However, when the *Course* says in Lesson 30, *"God is in everything I see because God is in my mind,"* it is not referring to seeing physical objects with one's eyes. It is instead talking about vision as it exists in reality. So in Lesson 30, it is explained, *"The idea for today is the springboard for vision. From this idea will the world open up before you, and you will look upon it and see in it what you have never seen before....Real vision is not limited to concepts such as 'near' and 'far'...real vision is not only unlimited by space and distance, but it does not depend on the body's eyes at all. The mind is its only source...."*

I decided it was now time to speak to a Hindu teacher, so I got on the tube and headed to South London. Set in the quiet and attractive leafy streets of Clapham South, is the London Satyananda Yoga Centre. Swami Pragyamurti is the yoga teacher or *acharya* who lives there and runs the centre. She is of Irish origin and now belongs to the Saraswati monastic order. She was initiated as a swami by her guru Swami Satyananda in 1979. It is interesting to note that Swami Satyananda was initiated himself at the age of 19 by the Indian saint and sage, Swami Sivananda Saraswati, to whom I have just referred.

Swami Pragyamurti told me that she was instructed by her guru to train yoga teachers. So she established the London Satyananda Yoga Centre in 1971 and it has progressed gradually since then. Today the Centre offers meditation classes, pranayama classes, which involve working with the breath, and classes in asanas

---

[112] *ACIM*, Lesson 29, W45.

or physical postures. She was kind enough to devote quite a bit of time to me and we had a long discussion, which I found so interesting that I would like to present it here in question and answer format.

RN: Could you start off please by telling me about *maya*?

SP: Well, on the one hand *maya* is interpreted as illusion but on the other hand we can consider it to be everything around us—this whole divine creation, the manifestation of the divine, all planets and everything that is in the universe. But I don't think all this can be called an illusion unless it is on condition that we understand the exact meaning of reality. Reality is one, constant and unchanging. Most of us spiritual seekers have no idea what that is and we just bandy words about, which seems to me to be distinctly unhelpful. To me my body is a reality. The trees, flowers, birds and squirrels in the garden are a reality. They may not be the ultimate reality but we must be very careful about how we bandy words about. Truly enlightened beings may talk about reality because they are the only ones who know about it. But for the rest of us to say nothing is real, it's all an illusion; this can lead us up and down all sorts of blind alleys and into unspiritual behaviour.

RN: So you are saying that the concept of illusion could be misused?

SP: Yes, and we could also misuse or abuse ourselves because of it. Personally, my prayer is to be able to live a loving and useful life.

RN: But don't you eventually want to take yourself off the karmic wheel of life, or repeated cycles of birth and death, and become enlightened?

SP: But why? I love life. I suppose ultimately I do want to become enlightened but I don't understand how one who professes to be on the Divine Path can turn his back on the divine creation because it is seen to be an illusion. This is a complete contradiction in terms. So for me, I would rather deal with what is my reality now, which is what I can aspire to and what I do understand.

RN: But enlightened beings have spoken about reality and we can learn from them.

SP: Of course we must listen to the words of the Masters but they have reached a different state of mind. Their minds are not limited like ours are. How can we understand this talk of the infinite with such limited minds?

RN: But don't you have some idea of what enlightenment means?

SP: There are only a few enlightened beings on this planet at the present time and they are here to help bring others to that state of oneness with themselves and with the divine. So I can aspire to that—to be of service— and I will continue from there, stage by stage. But no, I don't know what enlightenment means other than what I see in my own guru and in His Holiness the Dalai Lama and a few other great beings who are not looking to escape, but who are concerned with being of service to humanity and to reflect the perfection and glory of creation, I think.

RN: I agree that we should all try to be of service to humanity, if we can. But I think that pointing the way towards enlightenment is a service in a way—teaching people that what we have around us, however beautiful and wondrous it may be, is not the ultimate reality and that we should perhaps aspire to more than the world of phenomena.

SP: Maybe we should, but as long as we are doing so badly at just being nice to each other and to the planet, how can we?

RN: Yes, I would agree that that's where it starts—being nice to each other and to the planet. And, in fact, *A Course in Miracles* focuses on much more than being nice. It says we must forgive everyone and everything at all times. That's the very first step. Well, to turn to the topic of the ego, would you agree that overcoming the ego is an important factor in spiritual development?

SP: Yes, but as long as we live in a body, we've got an ego. The petty demands of the ego definitely can be modified and helped through the practices of meditation and other things, no doubt, as can our rather sad identification with various aspects of the ego, such as possessions, or looks or style.

RN: Are you referring to detachment then?

SP: I think I need to challenge all these classical spiritual precepts. Detachment from the little, unimportant things in our life—yes. But I have come to realise that I am a half decent human being because of my attachment to my children and various others whom I love. I think the gift of love that we are given as parents is the greatest spiritual teaching of all time. You know, if you're a mother, you can never put yourself first again—ever. So that is one heck of a kick to the ego and it comes through parenthood. Also the gift of unconditional love, another great spiritual teaching, comes to us through attachment to our children. So I am totally confused about detachment on one level.

RN: I must say I agree with you on that last point because I have a son whom I love deeply and I am attached to him in my mind and sometimes I do wonder whether that attachment will come between me and God. I am not sure...

SP: Yes, it is difficult, but I would rather become an atheist again than bow down to a God who tells me not to love my children.

RN: You mentioned meditation earlier. It is an important practice isn't it for spiritual seekers?

SP: Yes, but it requires patience. It's a long, long process and I think the essence of meditation and of all spiritual practice is that it helps us on our way to living loving, kind and useful lives and it takes us a little bit further on the road to freedom. So the fact that we sit for meditation is the point. What we must not do is to judge it and bemoan the fact that one is hopeless at meditating. Just be mindful of it and keep on meditating day after day.

RN: I suppose the aim of meditation is to rise above the thoughts that keep cropping up—to go beyond the intellect?

SP: Yes, and the only way to do that is not by fighting it. It's just by watching your thoughts, observing, being the witness and also to watch the spaces between the thought, so that the spaces get longer and the thoughts get fewer.

RN: Buddhist teachers and Hindu teachers all recommend meditation, don't they?

SP: Yes. Yogis and Buddhists are very close cousins and they all recommend meditation because it's about mindfulness. One of the sad things about yoga in the West is that, even after so many years since the 1960's, people are still stuck on asanas (physical postures.)

RN: You could in fact manage without asanas couldn't you?

SP: Yes, they are only a small part of yoga. If I ruled the world I would like meditation to be mandatory for everybody! Everybody should meditate every day.

RN: I would like to see school children meditating every day.

SP: I agree!

And with that, our long and thought-provoking discussion came to an end. As I made my way home on the tube, I thought a lot about that interesting and, at times, rather challenging conversation. So when I got home I decided to sit down and wade my way through *A Course in Miracles* to see if I could find answers to some of the issues that the conversation had brought up. I should add that I felt really grateful to Swami Pragyamurti for encouraging me in this way to delve deeper into the teachings of the *Course.*

Swami Pragyamurti had stressed how important it was to her to live a loving and useful life. *ACIM,* being the path of forgiveness, or the yoga of forgiveness, as I call it, stresses love too. Only a loving heart can forgive, so love *is* at the foundation of all the teachings of the *Course.* It calls on us to love each other because we are all joined—we are all one with each other and one with God and it calls on us to be grateful because of this. Lesson 195 in the Workbook states, *"Love is the way I walk in gratitude,"* and it is explained in that lesson that, *"We thank our Father for one thing alone; that we are separate from no living thing, and therefore one with Him....Our gratitude will pave the way to Him, and shorten our learning time by more than you could ever dream of. Gratitude goes hand in hand with love, and where one is the other must be found. For gratitude is but an aspect of the Love which is the Source of all creation."* [113]

---

[113] *ACIM,* W373, Lesson 195.

Concerning the curriculum of the Holy Spirit, the Voice for God, who is the Guide provided by God for us since the time of the separation, the *Course* emphasises that this curriculum is based on love and forgiveness. *"Every loving thought is true. Everything else is an appeal for healing and help, regardless of the form it takes."* [114] And further on in the Text we read, *"And now the reason why you are afraid of this Course should be apparent. For this is a Course on love, because it is about you. You have been told that your function in this world is healing, and your function in Heaven is creating. The ego teaches that your function on earth is destruction, and you have no function at all in Heaven.... I have said you have but two emotions, love and fear. One is changeless but continually exchanged, being offered by the eternal to the eternal. In this exchange it is extended, for it increases as it is given. The other has many forms, for the content of individual illusions differs greatly. Yet they have one thing in common; they are all insane."* [115] And the following prayer, which is one of my favourites, is all about love:

> *Father, I wake today with miracles correcting my perception of all things. And so begins the day I share with You as I will share eternity, for time has stepped aside today. I do not seek the things of time, and so I will not look upon them. What I seek today transcends all laws of time and things perceived in time. I would forget all things except Your Love. I would abide in You, and know no laws except Your law of love. And I would find the peace which You created for Your Son, forgetting all the foolish toys I made as I behold Your glory and my own."* [116]

One very relevant issue was raised in the interview at the London Satyananda Yoga Centre. Swami Pragyamurti pointed out that she didn't know what reality is and no one does, except for the enlightened Masters. I would agree with her, and this is what we read in *ACIM*. *"The definition of reality is God's, not yours. He created it and He knows what it is. You who knew have forgotten, and unless He had given you a way to remember you would have condemned yourself to oblivion. Because of your Father's Love you can never forget Him, for no one can forget*

---

[114] *ACIM*, T215.
[115] *ACIM*, T245 & T247.
[116] *ACIM*, W476, Lesson 346.

what God Himself placed in his memory. You can deny it, but you cannot lose it. A Voice will answer every question you ask, and a vision will correct the perception of everything you see." That voice is the Voice of the Holy Spirit. We *can* ask Him to teach us about reality. If we ask, He will answer.

Love of one's children was another topic that cropped up in the interview with Swami Pragyamurti and I realised, after browsing through the *Course* numerous times, that it does not call on us to relinquish or detach from the love we feel as parents for our children. But it goes much further than simple mother/child love. The *Course* tells us we should love *everyone* as we love our children—at least that is my interpretation of the following passage. *"You cannot enter into real relationships with any of God's Sons unless you love them all and equally. Love is not special. If you single out part of the Sonship for your love, you are imposing guilt on all your relationships and making them unreal. You can only love as God loves. Seek not to love unlike Him, for there is no love apart from His. Until you recognize that this is true, you will have no idea what love is like."* [117] So not only should I love my son, but I should love everyone else as much as I love him. That will take a lot of working towards but it might help me if I remember this, as I go about my daily life and meet all sorts of people—some very loveable but some not so endearing! And if you ponder upon those words they do make sense. God loves all his creation equally—all his sons (and daughters.) As we have been created by Him, we must have similar characteristics and so when we love, we should really love as He does.

ACIM refers to the "strength" of love and that is something I can relate to. *"Only love is strong because it is undivided. The strong do not attack because they see no need to do so. Before the idea of attack can enter your mind, you must have perceived yourself as weak...."* [118] I really believe that strength comes through love and forgiveness. Whenever I read about Jesus I am always struck by his love and compassion and at the same time he always seems to me to exude great strength. His strength is a product of his loving heart. We all tend to think that fear-based actions like aggression, violence and war are signs of strength. Actually, they are

---

[117] *ACIM*, T265.
[118] *ACIM*, T225.

the exact opposite. They demonstrate fear and vulnerability. One strikes another for fear of being hurt and out of a lack of trust. These ego-based actions are really a sign of weakness. And if all of us— people and nations—had the inner strength that comes from a loving heart, and expressed this in our daily lives through tolerance, trust, understanding and forgiveness, there would be no need for fear-based acts of belligerence, war, hate, etc. Fear would be conquered if only we could let love prevail. Yes, I know I sound like a 1960's hippy and that it will take several hundreds of years for the peoples of the world to come to understand each other and accept their differences, thereby eradicating fear and mistrust. But we have to begin somewhere and at some time. I am convinced that the time is now and the place is within our own hearts. These words will resonate with those who are ready to practise love and forgiveness and I think their numbers are greater than one would imagine. Such people can be found in all countries of the world. How nice it would be to have a global army of love instead of our silly, little ego-dominated separate armies of hate, which kill and cause massive destruction purely out of fear or self-interest.

But before we can expect to see love on a global scale, we need to raise our children properly, so that we feel safe walking in the streets of our cities at night, without the dread of bumping into a gang of hooded teenagers. So before we look at other people and other countries we need to look within our own societies and our own homes and ask a few very pertinent questions. Am I giving my child enough love, attention and guidance? Am I teaching him right from wrong? Do I respect him and build up his self-esteem? Am I bringing into the world a young person who has a loving heart, honesty, integrity and a sense of responsibility? If not, then I have absolutely no right to give birth to a single child. In fact, I believe mothers (especially in the West where their economic needs are more or less secure) are indirectly responsible for most of the violence, substance abuse and lack of respect youngsters exhibit these days. Why pick on mothers? Because when it comes down to it, it *is* the mother, in the vast majority of cases, who raises her children, who spends the most time with them and who has the major role of nurturing them. Even today when both parents work, I feel that children are more willing to turn to their mothers for guidance and love, than they are to their fathers. Yes, there are some families in which fathers do a brilliant job, but those are in the minority.

In order for a teenager to treat others with respect and politeness he has to receive the same at home. His self esteem has to be bolstered through love, attention, praise and respect from his parents. If he doesn't get these, then his parents need to accept the responsibility for any trouble he may get into when he grows up. Also, I think the first seven years are crucial. If a child is to be brought up with a moral code, with a sense of right and wrong or with a belief in a religion or some form of spirituality, these things have to be instilled in him in the first seven years of his life. Parents who cannot do this have no right to reproduce. There is no shortage of contraceptive devices and there's no excuse for bad parenting, which is at the root of society's evils in the Western world. One may think up excuses, such as difficult economic circumstances or being a single parent for instance, but love doesn't cost anything and some single parents have brought beautifully-behaved children into the world, who grow up to become responsible citizens of integrity.

I often wonder why so many people reproduce—people who can barely look after themselves, never mind be expected to raise their children properly. In fact, given how overpopulated our planet is and how our vital resources are dwindling at an alarming rate, those who elect not to have children are doing the planet and all of us a favour. Sometimes I think people have babies just because everyone else does and they don't really give the matter much thought. Having a child is such a responsibility and a long-term commitment, and I can't help feeling that some people may not be aware of these considerations when they embark upon raising a family. On the other hand, I know many couples who *are* dedicated parents and who put their children's needs before their own.

Well I have gone off at a tangent and I hope the reader will forgive me, but bringing children up properly is a topic I feel very strongly about. I would like to pick up another point mentioned by the yoga teacher, Swami Pragyamurti. She said service to humanity is vital. I am sure everyone agrees with that. *ACIM* asks students of the *Course* to become "God's teachers" so that they can be of service to humanity. The form of service mentioned in the *Course* is to show the way to others, to awaken them from the illusions of the reality they perceive with their physical senses. Furthermore, as I mentioned previously although *ACIM* reiterates that the manifest world is an illusion, it does *not* deny the reality of the world or of the physical body to us human beings. But it says the body and the world have only one purpose. *"Yet what makes God's teachers is their recognition of the proper purpose of the body as they advance in their profession, they become more and more certain that the body's function is but to let God's Voice speak through it to human ears....The text explains that the Holy Spirit is the Answer to all problems you have made. These problems are not real, but that is meaningless to those who believe in them. And everyone believes in what he made, for it was made by his believing it. Into this strange and paradoxical situation—one without meaning and devoid of sense, yet out of which no way seems possible—God has sent His Judgment to answer yours."* [119] And then it is explained that God's Judgement is peace and peace *is* possible on earth if we follow the guidance of the Holy Spirit. As for the purpose of the world, it is given to us on page 36 of the *Manual for Teachers*. *"Until forgiveness is complete, the world does have a purpose. It becomes the home in which forgiveness is born, and where it grows and becomes stronger and more all-embracing."* So our service to humanity is to learn how to become forgiving—completely forgiving to everyone at all times.

If the world is an illusion why bother about anything? Why bother about myself or others? Why don't I just go to pieces, go out and harm others, commit suicide even? There are a number of good reasons why one definitely should not. Firstly, belief that the body is an illusion should not lead one to abuse or neglect one's body or health, because as long as we are living in a body and believe that, then it does have a function. The purpose is the one I just quoted above, *"....to let God's Voice speak through it to human ears."* We are also told, elsewhere in *ACIM*, that the body is a *"learning device"* for the mind. But whilst we do need to look after our bodies and live a healthy lifestyle so that they can be used for God's purpose, we don't really need to *focus on* the body or on appearances because ultimately the body isn't there.

Let me give an extreme example of another reason why I need to look after myself. If I harmed my illusory body through alcohol, drugs, excessive food or a near starvation diet, it would mean that I was "attacking" myself (to use the terminology of the *Course*.) In attacking myself it is clear that I do not forgive

---

[119] *ACIM*, M31 & M29.

myself for the original "sin" of separation that is in my sub-conscious mind. Thus I have *not* learned what the *Course* is teaching and therefore I cannot guide others in their spiritual quest, which is my only true function here on earth. So even though my body is not real, as long as it appears to be real to me, I think it is advisable to feed it healthy food and vitamins, to exercise regularly and meditate.   But whilst doing this I must constantly remember this important lesson, *"I am not a body, I am free. For I am still as God created me."* [120]

As for harming others, it is abundantly clear that the *Course* is asking us to do the exact opposite. We are asked to love and forgive every single being on this planet. I would also like to make a comment about suicide because a friend asked me once, *"Well, if it is all an illusion and forgiveness is the way out, why not just forgive everyone you know and then take your own life?"* I was taken aback a bit and didn't know how to answer that question immediately. But I gave it a lot of thought and realised that it's no use going around just saying, "I forgive you" to everyone. You have to *really mean it* and demonstrate it in all circumstances. Plus, there must be a great deal of emotional baggage tied in with the past, in one's mind, that also needs forgiving as well as the need to forgive oneself and I don't think this can be done in an instant. It takes dedicated hard work and constant requests to the Holy Spirit for guidance and for help in turning one's thoughts to right-mindedness and of living completely in the present and overlooking anything irritating. That's quite a tall order. But there is something else to consider. Forgiveness, according to the *Course,* does not mean overlooking an error on the part of someone else. It means recognising that *there has been no error* because life on earth is as real as a dream. I will explain more about that in Chapter 9.

As for suicide, it is no escape because when the body dies the ego lives on. It lives on until all its fears, guilt and desires have been wiped out. So if one hasn't learnt all the forgiveness lessons that have to be learnt, then death will simply result in rebirth in yet another illusory body. Suicide would impede one's spiritual progress because it would be putting off until the next lifetime, lessons that could have been learnt in the present lifetime. As stated above, *"Until*

---

[120] *ACIM,* W388, Lesson 201.

forgiveness is complete, the world...becomes the home in which forgiveness is born...."

The enlightened yogi Paramahansa Yogananda (1893-1952), in his well known book *Autobiography of a Yogi*, mentions the fact that death is no escape from the world of phenomena. He said his own guru Swami Sri Yukteswar explained to him that man has three lower bodies: the gross physical body, the astral body or body of desires, and the causal body or body of perception. When death removes the physical body, the astral and causal bodies still remain. He explains that it is only by overcoming desire that all three bodies can disintegrate and thereby bring about liberation for the soul. So it is clear that desire and ignorance are responsible for keeping us trapped in the world of samsara and death is no escape from them.

Ignorance is also mentioned in the famous *Yoga Sutras of Patanjali*. In the section on the practice of concentration it is explained in the commentary that, *"Through ignorance we have joined ourselves with a particular body, and thus opened ourselves to misery. This idea of a body is a simple superstition....According to Yoga philosophy, it is through ignorance that the soul has been joined with nature. The aim is to get rid of nature's control over us. That is the goal of all religions. Each soul is potentially divine...The body is just the external crust of the mind. They are not two different things; they are but two aspects of one thing; the internal substance of the oyster takes up matter from outside, and manufactures the shell. In the same way the internal fine forces which are called mind take up gross matter from outside, and from that manufacture this external shell, the body. If, then, we have control of the internal, it is very easy to have control of the external."* [121]

The way that the mind is controlled according to Hindu teachers is through meditation, breath control or *pranayama*, devotion to God, service to humanity and also through knowledge or *jnana* yoga, which I spoke about earlier in this chapter. Knowledge will enable us to discriminate between the real and the unreal, between reality and the world of phenomena or the world of illusions. Knowledge is the opposite of ignorance. If it is ignorance that is keeping us trapped in the cycle of birth, death and rebirth, then it must be knowledge that

---

[121] Swami Vivekananda, *The Yoga Sutras of Patanjali*, pp. 103-105, Sacred Texts, Watkins Publishing, London, 2007.

leads us to freedom. But, as the *Course* insists, knowledge about reality is not enough. The most important thing is to practise forgiveness.

Of all the Hindu sages that I have explored I think it is true to say that the teachings of Adi Sankara (788 - 820 AD) approximate the closest to the teachings of *ACIM*. Sankara (also known as Shankara or Sankaracharya) was an Indian philosopher who consolidated the teachings of the Advaita Vedanta. He preached pure non-duality and believed that there is only one Creator, Brahman, and nothing else has any reality. Sankara wrote commentaries on the Upanishads, on the Brahma Sutras and on the *Bhagavad Gita*. In one of his works, the *Crest-Jewel of Discrimination* (also known as *The Crest-Jewel of Wisdom*), he made it quite clear that the body is what stands between the individual soul and liberation. Speaking of the gross body he said, "*Compounded of skin, blood, flesh, fat, marrow, excreta, and urine, it is most filthy...cease also to associate the Self in any way with the body of skin, flesh, and bones. Make every effort to root out this error and holding fast to the knowledge of reality as the absolute Brahman, destroy the mind and obtain supreme peace. Then you will have no more births. Even a learned scholar who perfectly understands the meaning of Vedanta has no hope of liberation if, owing to delusion, he cannot give up the idea of the non-existent body as the Self.*" [122] So we see that knowledge of the scriptures will not help unless one is able to discriminate between the unreal and the real, i.e., the unreal physical or gross body and real self or spirit that was created by God or Brahman and *is one with Him*.

I would like to quote a few more of Sankara's words of wisdom. The following verses are from a different version of *The Crest-Jewel of Wisdom*.

> *As long as the Self is in bondage to the false personal self of evil,*
> *so long is there not even a possibility of freedom, for these two*
> *are contraries.*

> *But when free from the grasp of selfish personality, he reaches*
> *his real nature; Bliss and Being shine forth by their own light,*
> *like the full moon, free from blackness.*

---

[122] Ramana Maharshi and Shankara, *Ramana, Shankara and the Forty Verses, The Essential Teachings of Advaita*, pp. 32-33, Watkins Publishing, London, 2002.

But he who in the body thinks "this am I," a delusion built up by the mind through darkness; when this delusion is destroyed for him without remainder, there arises for him the realization of Self as the Eternal, free from all bondage.

The ascetic, who has put away the cause of bondage–attachment to the unreal–stands in the vision of the Self, saying, "this Self am I"; this resting in the Eternal, brings joy by experiencing it, and takes away the supreme sorrow that we feel, whose cause is unwisdom.

There is no freedom for him who is full of attachment to the body and its like; for him who is free, there is no wish for the body and its like; the dreamer is not awake, he who is awake dreams not; for these things are the opposites of each other.

Cut off all hope in sensual objects which are like poison, the cause of death; abandon all fancies of birth and family and social state; put all ritual actions far away; renounce the illusion of self -dwelling in the body, center the consciousness on the Self. Thou art the seer, thou art the stainless, thou art in truth the supreme, secondless Eternal.[123]

It is clear that the *"false personal self of evil"* and the *"selfish personality"* in the Sankara's verses above are references to the ego. Furthermore, it is interesting to note that he says the body was created by the mind *"through darkness,"* which can be compared to the wrong portion of the mind miscreating the body at the time of the separation or the splitting of the mind, as stated in *ACIM*. Also *"attachment to the unreal"* is deemed to be the cause of bondage, just as attachment to the ego is what stands in the way of liberation, according to *ACIM*. And in the fifth verse quoted above we see the same emphasis on the holiness and divinity of the real self as we see in the *Course*.

---

[123] Adi Sankara, *The Crest-Jewel of Wisdom*, Section entitled *The Power of Mind Images*, verses 299, 300, 301, 333, 337, 377, www.sacred-texts.com/hin/cjw/cjw09.htm.

Finally, here are a few more verses from another section of *The Crest-Jewel of Wisdom:*

> *The belief in this world is built up of unreality. In the one substance, changeless, formless, undifferentiated, what separateness can exist?*

> *In the one substance, in which no difference of seer, seeing, seen, exists, which is changeless, formless, undifferentiated, what separateness can exist?*

> *He who perceives that his soul's pilgrimage is ended, who is free from disunion even while possessing division, whose imagination is free from imaginings, he, verily, is called free even in life.*

> *He who even while this body exists, regards it as a shadow, who has no sense of personality or possessions–these are the marks of him who is free in life.*

> *Whose mind lingers not over the past, nor goes out after the future, when perfect equanimity is gained, this is the mark of him who is free even in life.*

> *He who has discerned the Eternal in the Self, through the power of sacred books, who is free from the bondage of the world, bears the mark of one who is free even in life.* [124]

The fourth verse refers to the need to have *"no sense of personality or possessions,"* which means overcoming the ego because it is the ego that gives us our sense of personality and that encourages us to cling to possessions. In the fifth verse just quoted we are advised to live in the present and pay no attention to the past or to the future, as well as to discriminate between the real self and

---

[124] Adi Sankara, *The Crest-Jewel of Wisdom,* Section entitled *Free Even in Life,* verses 399, 400, 429, 430, 431, 436, www.sacred-texts.com/hin/cjw/cjw10.htm.

the unreal, if we wish to attain liberation. And what is interesting is that when Sankara refers to the words *"free even in life,"* he is referring to the individual having achieved liberation whilst still dwelling in the world of illusion or maya. *ACIM* teaches us that when we have learnt all our forgiveness lessons and have turned totally to the Holy Spirit, we will finally have achieved liberation whilst living in the *real world*. At that point the body will be meaningless to us even though we may still appear to be dwelling on earth in the physical plane.

What does the *Course* mean when it refers to the *"real world"*? It says, *"The real world holds a counterpart for each unhappy thought reflected in your world; a sure correction for the sights of fear and sounds of battle which your world contains. The real world shows a world seen differently, through quiet eyes and with a mind at peace. Nothing but rest is there. There are no cries of pain and sorrow heard, for nothing there remains outside forgiveness."* [125]

In the Text of ACIM there is mention of a bridge from our illusory world to the real world. Once we have crossed this bridge we will, initially, still be able to see the illusory physical body. *"Across the bridge it is so different! For a time the body is still seen, but not exclusively, as it is seen here....Once you have crossed the bridge, the value of the body is so diminished in your sight that you will see no need at all to magnify it. For you will realize that the only value the body has is to enable you to bring your brothers to the bridge with you, and to be released together there."* [126]

I think the stage of the *real world* is just before the stage of enlightenment or liberation. It certainly does seem like a long and arduous journey that lies in front of us. But judging by the following passage it will definitely be worth it when we get there in the end. *"This world of light, this circle of brightness is the real world, where guilt meets with forgiveness. Here the world outside is seen anew, without the shadow of guilt upon it. Here are you forgiven, for here you have forgiven everyone. Here is the new perception, where everything is bright and shining with innocence, washed in the waters of forgiveness, and cleansed of every evil thought you laid upon it....We need remember only that whoever attains the real world, beyond which learning cannot go, will go beyond it, but in a different way. Where learning ends there God begins, for*

---

[125] *ACIM*, W443.
[126] *ACIM*, T346.

*learning ends before Him Who is complete where He begins, and where there **is** no end...."* [127] At this point the disciple has come to the end of his journey, having achieved liberation or *Samadhi.*

I would like to end with the following quotation from a book on Kundalini yoga entitled *Kundalini – The Mother of the Universe.* It is interesting because it shows that the ego or lower mind is equated with ignorance and illusion. The yogi overcomes the ego by controlling his mind; this could be through meditation, study, pranayama (breath control) or wise discrimination. By overcoming the ego he achieves liberation. *"The lower mind is ignorance itself. When the mind is controlled, ignorance, which is the Mother of Maya (illusion), dies. The Yogi attains Samadhi or the state of Brahma."* [128]

---

[127] *ACIM,* T395 & 396.

[128] Rishi Singh Gherwal, *Kundalini, The Mother of the Universe, The Mystery of Piercing the Six Chakras,* Chapter on *Samadhi Yoga,* 1930, www.sacred-texts.com/hin/kmu/kmu10.htm.

Chapter 4

More on Illusion

"Is all that we see or seem

but a dream within a dream?" [129]

Approximately 25% of those over 65 in Britain, or around 2.6 million people, are thought to be suffering from depression according to a 2008 study by Age Concern. This is a very sad statistic. For those living in care homes the situation is even worse, as 40% of these patients are thought to suffer from symptoms of depression. Age Concern's study reported that one of the symptoms of depression in the elderly is "a feeling that life is pointless." In a comment on *The Daily Telegraph* website one 83-year old said not having a future ahead and "no hope syndrome" were factors that contributed to depression. I think this is understandable. I can imagine that if I had just carried on with my life without having come across *ACIM* (or another Path), I too would have felt disheartened, if not depressed, as I grew older.

Depression, not only among the elderly but in all age groups, is understandable if one is wrapped up in the world of the ego, which really is a meaningless world. At least that's how I see it as I sit and ponder about the point of it all. Growing up, growing old and dying. Can there be any meaning in that? I sometimes become quite dejected when I think about it until I remember that it

---

[129] Edgar Allen Poe (1809 – 1849) poem entitled *A Dream within a Dream*.

isn't really happening!

I would like to refer to a passage from the *Course* that I mentioned in Chapter 1, *"Death is the central dream from which all illusions stem. Is it not madness to think of life as being born, aging, losing vitality, and dying in the end? ....It is the one fixed, unchangeable belief of the world that all things in it are born only to die. This is regarded as the 'way of nature,' not to be raised to question, but to be accepted as the 'natural' law of life...."* [130] I think it is madness not to question this and I think many other people feel the same way. Life doesn't make any sense to them either and they don't know what to do about it. But *ACIM* offers these words of encouragement, *"When you are sad, know this need not be. Depression comes from a sense of being deprived of something you want and do not have. Remember that you are deprived of nothing except by your own decisions, and then decide otherwise."* [131]

As we grow older we want life to be as it used to be and, as we see it rapidly dwindling away from us, we want to hold on to it. We want it to last forever but we know it won't. But if we realise that everything in the world of phenomena, the world created by the ego, cannot possibly last, then perhaps we will start looking for ways of transcending this world and aspiring to eternal life. The way to do that is to overcome the ego and the *Course's* technique for this is forgiveness.

The denial of God, or the divine spark, in oneself and in others is one of the causes of depression. *"Depression means that you have forsworn God....Do not forget, however, that to deny God will inevitably result in projection, and you will believe that others and not yourself have done this to you...Do not attribute your denial of joy to them, or you cannot see the spark in them that would bring joy to you. It is the denial of the spark that brings depression, for whenever you see your brothers without it, you are denying God."* [132] According to the *Course*, the remedy for this problem is to embrace the world of God and, as mentioned above, overcome the ego. The result of this would be a definite remedy for depression, as one can see by the following passage: *"O my child, if you knew what God wills for you, your joy would be*

---

[130] *ACIM,* M66.

[131] *ACIM,* T63.

[132] *ACIM,* T189.

complete. And what He wills has happened, for it was always true. When the light comes and you have said, 'God's Will is mine,' you will see such beauty that you will know it is not of you. Out of your joy you will create beauty in His Name, for your joy could no more be contained than His. The bleak little world (of the ego) will vanish into nothingness, and your heart will be so filled with joy that it will leap into Heaven, and into the Presence of God. I can tell you, and remind you often, that what God wills for Himself He wills for you, and what He wills for you is yours." [133] How beautiful and inspiring those words are. One can actually see joy and peace on the faces of those who have managed to transcend the ego—the Dalai Lama springs to mind. He always looks peaceful, happy and serene.

I fell in love with the following poem when I came across it one day and have read it over and over again. It is so uplifting. I am convinced that the American, Rosicrucian writer, poet and mystic, Ella Wheeler Wilcox was an avant-garde *A Course in Miracles* student.

KNOW THE ONE, BY KNOWING THAT NOTHING ELSE REMAINS TO BE KNOWN [134]

God and I in space alone and nobody else in view.

"And where are the people, O Lord," I said,

"the earth below and the sky o'er head

and the dead whom once I knew?"

"That was a dream," God smiled and said,

"A dream that seemed to be true.

---

[133] *ACIM,* T199.

[134] www.geocities.com/radhakutir. This poem was published in *Rays From The Rose Cross,* the Rosicrucian Fellowship Magazine in July 1959.

There were no people, living or dead,

there was no earth, and no sky o'er head;

there was only Myself – in you."

"Why do I feel no fear," I asked,

"meeting You here this way?

For I have sinned I know full well –

and is there heaven, and is there hell,

and is this the Judgment Day?"

"Nay, those were but dreams,"

the Great God said,

"Dreams that have ceased to be.

There are no such things as fear or sin;

there is no you – you never have been –

there is nothing at all but Me."

by Ella Wheeler Wilcox

1850 – 1919

She has also been quoted as saying:

So many gods, so many creeds!

So many paths that wind and wind,

When just the art of being kind,

Is all this sad world needs."

And that too could be a *Course* saying, especially if one substitutes the word *forgiving* for the word *kind*. If one forgives one *is* kind. If one is kind, one forgives.

"Spirit is the real and eternal; matter is the unreal and temporal." That was a quotation by Mary Baker Eddy (1821–1910) the founder of the Christian Science movement. It is interesting to note that some of the teachings of this movement conform quite closely to those of *ACIM*. Christian Scientists believe in One God/One Mind and that God is Divine Love; the true nature of human beings is spiritual and they are all part of God. God is all that exists and He has no knowledge of disease, evil, death, etc.; all disease is caused by the mind and people can heal themselves by joining with Him in their minds. *"When the thinker is lost in the eminence of Mind the healing takes place."* [135]

This is what *ACIM* has to say about sickness: *"The ego has a profound investment in sickness. If you are sick, how can you object to the ego's firm belief that you are not invulnerable? ....Sickness is a way of demonstrating that you can be hurt. It is a witness to your frailty, your vulnerability, and your extreme need to depend on external guidance. The ego uses this as its best argument for your need for **its** guidance....All sickness comes from separation. When the separation is denied, it goes. For it is gone as soon as the idea that brought it has been healed, and been replaced by sanity....A broken body shows the mind has not been healed. A miracle of healing proves that separation is without effect....Healing is the result of using the body solely for communication. Since this is natural it heals by making whole, which is also natural. All mind is whole, and the belief that part of it is physical, or not mind, is a fragmented or sick interpretation...."* [136] (The reference here to communication refers to using the body to enable the Holy Spirit to communicate through it to others.)

Why is it that all living creatures become ill? Humans and animals all succumb to disease, and the very few that don't, still face death in the end, which can be put into the same category as disease. Infants, children, young people, adults and the elderly—we all get sick, even if we live healthy lifestyles, eat our five daily portions of fruit and vegetables, take supplements and exercise. Why is the health industry doing such a roaring trade? Why has the alternative health

---

[135] Mary Baker Eddy, quotation from www.mbeinstitute.org.
[136] *ACIM*, T155, 156, 554, 569, 153.

industry burgeoned in recent years? Why do we all need to be healed by one means or another? It is because our *minds* are sick. They are sick because they are following the ego's teachings about the body. The ego sees the body as an end in itself simply because the body is the temple of the ego and was created by the ego as a place of refuge. But we should remember that, *"All mind is whole, and the belief that part of it is physical, or not mind, is a fragmented or sick interpretation. Mind cannot be made physical, but it can be made manifest through the physical if it uses the body to go beyond itself. By reaching out the mind extends itself. It does not stop at the body, for if it does it is blocked in its purpose. A mind that has been blocked has allowed itself to be vulnerable to attack, because it has turned against itself."* [137] The trouble is that we all believe we are bodies because we know no better. The body *seems* real and it certainly causes us enough pain to make sure we remember that it is real, but *ACIM* keeps insisting that it is not. It is this recognition that should pave the way to good health. But we need to open up our minds to this belief or, in the terminology of the *Course*, we need to remove the blocks that exist in the mind. *"The removal of blocks, then, is the only way to guarantee help and healing. Help and healing are the normal expressions of a mind that is working through the body, but not* ***in*** *it...Perceiving the body as a separate entity cannot but foster illness, because it is not true."* [138] Then the *Course* goes on to explain that the body should be used as a means of communication and that should be its *only function*. This will lead to good health. But if we think that the body has other functions this will lead to confusion and cause ill health, especially if the body is used to attack others in any way.

In her book *Science and Health* Mary Baker Eddy wrote, *"All reality is in God and His creation, harmonious and eternal. That which He creates is good, and He makes all that is made. Therefore the only reality of sin, sickness, or death is the awful fact that unrealities seem real to human, erring belief, until God strips off their disguise."* And speaking of traditional means of healing she wrote, *"Then comes the question, how do drugs, hygiene, and animal magnetism heal? It may be affirmed that they do not heal, but only relieve suffering temporarily, exchanging one disease for another. We classify disease as error, which nothing but Truth or Mind can heal, and this Mind must be*

---

[137] *ACIM*, T153.
[138] *ACIM*, T153.

divine, not human. Mind transcends all other power, and will ultimately supersede all other means in healing." [139] We can see that both the *Course* and Christian Science believe that sickness is error and can only be healed at the level of the mind, i.e., divine mind. *ACIM* says healing of the mind takes place when one accepts the Atonement, which has the effect of cancelling out all errors.

As for the human body, Mary Baker Eddy had this to say, *"There is no life, truth, intelligence, nor substance in matter. All is infinite Mind and its infinite manifestation, for God is All-in-all. Spirit is immortal Truth; matter is mortal error. Spirit is the real and eternal, matter is the unreal and temporal. Spirit is God, and man is His image and likeness. Therefore man is not material; he is spiritual."* This is practically the same belief as the *Course*.

About 20 years ago a friend gave me a copy of a book entitled *Spiritual Interpretation of Scripture* by the Christian Science practitioner Joel Goldsmith (1892–1964.) I read it and enjoyed it but I don't think I really understood some of the things that wise mystic was saying. Then after studying the *Course* I decided to peer inside the book again. This time I couldn't put it down! Now everything he spoke about makes much more sense and the similarity with the *Course* is amazing. It was as though he, in 1947, was already aware of some of the information that was to be given to Helen Schucman, the scribe of *ACIM*, in the 1970's. Let me quote a few passages so the reader can see what I mean.

Goldsmith insists that God did not create the physical world. He refers to the statement by Jesus in the Bible, *"My kingdom is not of this world,"* [140] and explains, *"'My kingdom' means the realm of Spirit, Soul, or I AM; 'this world' means the universe of concepts; the illusion or mirage. It naturally follows that this means there is nothing of 'My kingdom', of the Christ in 'this world'—the universe we see, hear, taste, touch or smell. To you and to me, this is the most tremendous revelation in the Bible. It shows us why there are wars with all their horrors of disaster, wreck, ruin, wounds, insanity, death and destruction—and God does nothing about it."* [141] When I read that paragraph all

---

[139] Mary Baker Eddy, *Science & Health,* p. 472, 24 – 27 & p. 483, 1 – 6, www.mbeinstitute.org.
[140] King James Bible, *John,* 18:36.
[141] Joel S Goldsmith, *Spiritual Interpretation of Scripture,* pp. 125-126, Willing Publishing Company, San Gabriel, California, 1969.

those years ago I completely misunderstood it. I thought it meant that God does not intervene to prevent wars from happening because He gave man free will. Well, I still believe God gave us free will but that is not what this paragraph is getting at. The reason God does nothing about it is because He is not aware of what is happening. He is not aware because this world is an illusion, a mirage, and God is not even aware that it exists in our minds, or in the lower part or wrong part of our minds, to be more precise.

Goldsmith continues with the following advice, *"You must see and understand 'this world' as a mirage, an illusion, a mesmeric suggestion and not attempt to heal it, pray for it, save it or redeem it; but see it for what it is—a false concept of Reality, a dream-picture."* And he says spiritual seekers should ignore things like politics and anything else related to this world of ours and instead, *"Your endeavour now is to cease from consideration of the things of 'this world,' so as to tune in on the beam that leads to the realization of 'My kingdom."* [142] In other words, the way to liberation is to recognise this world for what it is—unreal—and to focus on the only real world, the world of spirit.

Speaking about the reason why there is so much conflict in the world, Goldsmith made the following perceptive comment on page 157 of his book, *"... we have never had peace in the world and this in spite of all the thousands of religions that are on earth. All of these have failed to bring about the condition of peace—and for one reason: they have failed to emphasize the oneness of the individual and God. When we realize this oneness we realize this is the true relationship in the world. There is no longer any need for war."* And he went on to say that there would also be no need for racial or religious prejudice, bigotry or envy.

Further on in his book, on page 205, Goldsmith points out that our world is no part of God and he says, *"Be assured that if God were in this scene there would be no wars, accidents, diseases or deaths. God, the infinite Power of good, is able to maintain harmoniously and eternally Its own creation."* And that makes perfect sense and may help people understand why God does not intervene to prevent all the misfortune and calamities that afflict us and our planet.

As a Christian Scientist, Joel Goldsmith dealt, of course, with the topic of

---

[142] Ibid., pp. 127-128.

spiritual healing in his book. *"Nothing goes from the practitioner* (healer) *to God or from the practitioner to the patient. God, practitioner and patient are all one.... Until the three become one, the treatment is not complete; as long as there is a sense of duality, the treatment is not complete."* And he explains that if we all recognised our oneness with God, i.e., believed in pure non-duality, we would not get ill. *"The reason we lose our sense of oneness is because of a universal sense of mesmerism. All forms of daily life are presenting pictures of good and evil—newspapers, pictures, novels, etc. All of this suggestion seems to set up in us a sense of separation, discord, lack. Re-establish the sense of oneness—this is all there is to meditation or treatment."* [143] In other words, if we become aware of the illusory nature of the world and are able to experience our oneness with God (and for this, Goldsmith strongly recommended meditation) then we will no longer suffer from any ill health.

Goldsmith spoke about the Second Coming of Christ and gave it a completely different meaning from the view of orthodox Christianity. He said, *"The coming of Christ is the coming of perfection in you and in me—not the coming of a man who would be perfect... we have to become a full and complete living Christ."* [144] Compare this to what is said in *ACIM* regarding the Second Coming, *"Christ's Second Coming, which is sure as God, is merely the correction of mistakes, and the return of sanity. It is a part of the condition that restores the never lost, and re-establishes what is forever and forever true. It is the willingness to let forgiveness rest upon all things without exception and without reserve....The Second Coming is the time in which all minds are given to the hands of Christ, to be returned to spirit in the name of true creation and the Will of God...."* [145]

Both Goldsmith and the *Course* are saying the same thing, i.e., that the Second Coming refers to the time when we *all* will have become as perfect as Christ. It is a collective, internal experience rather than the external appearance of Christ on earth for the second time. *ACIM* tells us that we can achieve this if we become completely loving and forgiving. Goldsmith tells us that we can achieve this by meditating in the way that he taught, i.e., by focusing on the phrase, *"I and the*

---

[143] Joel S Goldsmith, *Spiritual Interpretation of Scripture*, pp. 138–140, Willing Publishing Company, San Gabriel, California, 1969.

[144] Ibid., p.161.

[145] *ACIM*, W449.

Father are one." Similarly, if we turn to Lesson 124 in *ACIM* we read, *"Let me remember I am one with God"*; Lesson 36, *"My mind is part of God's. I am very holy;* and Lesson 95, *"I am one Self, united with my Creator."*

Goldsmith also said, *"A God in heaven does us no good—we must feel it inside. There is no error except the belief in separation from God. Duality is the only devil."* [146] *ACIM* says practically the same thing: *"The mind can make the belief in separation very real and very fearful, and this belief is the 'devil.'"* [147] And how is the "devil" overcome? *"Forgiveness is the healing of the perception of separation."* [148] Thus by healing the perception of separation we overcome duality.

I would now like to deal with the topic of prayer. We normally pray to God when we are worried about something or someone, such as when a loved one is really ill; when we want something to change, such as having more money or finding a new partner or a new job; or when we are happy with what has been given us, such as winning something or other. So prayer in the traditional sense is each of us talking to God and asking Him to intervene to solve a problem or thanking Him for something. But is this really what prayer is all about? If, as the *Course* tells us, God is unaware of us living in our self-made illusory world, would it be possible for Him to intervene on our behalf? Hardly.

For Goldsmith prayer consists of listening to God, *"Prayer is not what goes from the individual to God—but that which comes from God the universal, to the individual consciousness. Prayer is the Word of God which comes to you in Silence...To me, prayer is a state of receptivity in which Truth is realized without taking conscious thought."* So prayer is more like meditation—we sit quietly and listen. We don't ask for anything. This is what Goldsmith had to say about traditional prayer: *"Prayers uttered for the purpose of healing, improving or aiding the people or conditions of the physical universe, reach no farther than one's own belief and bring only the results of our belief."*

What does the Course tell us about prayer? *"Prayer is a way of asking for*

---

[146] Joel S Goldsmith, *Spiritual Interpretation of Scripture*, p. 145, Willing Publishing Company, San Gabriel, California, 1969.

[147] *ACIM*, T50.

[148] *ACIM*, T46.

something. It is the medium of miracles. But the only meaningful prayer is for forgiveness, because those who have been forgiven have everything. Once forgiveness has been accepted, prayer in the usual sense becomes utterly meaningless. The prayer for forgiveness is nothing more than a request that you may be able to recognize what you already have." [149]

Kenneth Wapnick, *ACIM* teacher and the author of numerous books, was asked about the effectiveness of praying for others. He said it was ineffective because, *"First, God does not have to be told what to do; it is simply insane to believe that. Second, and even more important...once we pray for others, we are saying there is a problem out there, and then we are right back in the ego's trap. We do not pray for others, we pray for ourselves—that our minds, which believed there was a form of darkness outside, be healed....We pray, really, for help to get ourselves out of the way, so that the Holy Spirit can extend through our mind to other minds."* [150]

The following is one of many prayers in Part II of the Workbook: *"Father, today I would but hear Your Voice. In deepest silence I would come to You, to hear Your Voice and to receive Your Word. I have no prayer but this: I come to You to ask You for the truth. And truth is but Your Will, which I would share with you today."* [151] I find those words so beautiful.

I would like to give the reader some background information on Joel Goldsmith before quoting the most important passage of his book. When his father was very close to death he was healed miraculously by a Christian Science practitioner. After this experience, Goldsmith turned to Christian Science himself. During World War I, he received a sort of personal message through the Bible. The Bible fell on the floor by his bed with a page open and a passage illuminated. That passage told him that he should pray not for his own nation but for the enemy. Ever since then Goldsmith did just that. Later on in his life he contracted TB and nearly died but was healed, just as his father had been, by a Christian Science practitioner. From then on he became a spiritual healer and

---

[149] *ACIM*, T45.

[150] Kenneth Wapnick, *The 50 Miracle Principles of A Course in Miracles,* p. 93, Temecula, CA, 2005, used by permission of the *Foundation for A Course in Miracles.*

[151] *ACIM*, W421, Lesson 254.

teacher and he travelled around the world healing and teaching his spiritual principles, which he called *The Infinite Way*.

To return for the last time to that gem of a book *Spiritual Interpretation of Scripture*, there was a passage in that book that did not make any sense to me when I read it 20 years ago. In fact, I put a big question mark next to it. But today, thanks to *ACIM*, I think I understand it perfectly. The passage in question states, *"The secret ... is this: The life which you behold in man, tree or animal is not the Life which is God; human, animal or plant life is not a manifestation of God, and therefore is not immortal, eternal or spiritual. The life of material man or flower is mortal sense objectified: it is a false sense of the Life which is real. The understanding of this truth ... will enable you to refrain from attempting to heal, correct or reform the mortal sense of existence... You cannot behold or experience external Life and its harmonies and beauties while accepting the evidence of the senses as if it were God's creation."* [152] I think that is as close as we can get to the teachings of *ACIM*. Goldsmith called it the *Great Revelation* and the *secret of secrets*. He said kings and emperors would give their thrones if they could but learn that one truth! And, on page 213, he asked a very relevant question, *"Can you imagine the power-drunk, the money-mad, the hoarder, the gluttons, understanding that what he is handling, saving, fighting and dying for—is shadow—mirage?"*

It certainly makes you stop and think about life, doesn't it? Knowing this "secret of secrets" has changed the way I look at life. When I hear news of a catastrophe or disaster such as a plane crash or people killed in war it still upsets me terribly and I often have to turn off the television. But as I watch the tragic images I sometimes withdraw myself, in my mind, as though I was observing a world that doesn't really exist. It is a sort of surreal feeling and is hard to describe. Then I wonder how I would feel if I were in that situation. It's a horrible thought, but I think that knowing it is all unreal and that the only reality is spirit makes it that little bit easier to bear. These words of the *Course* often repeat themselves in my mind, *"You made it up."* (I think it is advisable to minimise one's time in front of TV news bulletins though because of the

---

[152] Joel S Goldsmith, *Spiritual Interpretation of Scripture*, p. 211, Willing Publishing Company, San Gabriel, California, 1969.

emphasis on all that is horrible, painful and violent in our world today.)

When you awaken to the fact that it is all just an illusion, you may find you change in certain ways. Things that you used to do, places that you used to visit, people whom you used to socialise with and topics of discussion that used to stimulate you, may all no longer be as interesting as before. Personally speaking, I have become more of a recluse recently because the things I used to do just don't appeal to me anymore, e.g., going shopping; going out for a meal with friends; dating and searching for a partner; chatting about politics or religion; even travelling. They have all lost their significance to me. And as I sit at home watching television I often flick from one channel to another in search of something that would hold my attention.

I have never been one for spending a long time in front of the mirror but nowadays I try to spend no more than three or four minutes in the morning. I don't enjoy buying or wearing fancy clothes and could easily live in jeans and t-shirts. I have little interest in the latest fashion or jewellery. I have never enjoyed long telephone conversations but now I try to minimise them even more as I have come to the conclusion that we all talk too much and say very little. And I don't enjoy going to parties where I have to make small talk with complete strangers. I realise this is simply part of the inevitable "sorting out" process that is mentioned in *ACIM* as I adjust to a totally new way of looking at the world. Fortunately, there are still a few things I do enjoy, such as wandering on my own through the forest or along the sea shore, spending time with my son and my cat, reading, cooking, watching comedies and old black and white movies on television and listening to music.

"Nine-tenths of the ideas which occupy our thoughts, which are the subjects of our conversations, discussions, discourses, public and private, have no existence in Reality," [153] said the wise philosopher Wei Wu Wei. With reference to serious topics of discussion he had this to say, *"When you hear someone speaking in all earnestness of the benefits of industrialisation, of social services, of democracy... or of abstract notions such as Justice, Liberty, Nationalism, Equality, do you think of them as real things or do*

---

[153] Wei Wu Wei *Fingers Pointing towards the Moon*, p. 12, First Sentient Publications, Colorado, USA, 2003.

you smile?.... if you have come to revalue values then you perceive their total unreality....Our values change as we grow up." [154]

I came across a similar view to Wei Wu Wei's in *ACIM*: *"You do not know the meaning of anything you perceive. Not one thought you hold is wholly true. The recognition of this is your firm beginning. You are not misguided; you have accepted no guide at all. Instruction in perception is your great need, for you understand nothing."* [155] *ACIM* also tells us that as an individual makes progress with its teachings he will go through various periods of adjustment and, *"...having learned that the changes in his life are always helpful, he must now decide all things on the basis of whether they increase the helpfulness or hamper it. He will find that many, if not most of the things he valued before will merely hinder his ability to transfer what he has learned to new situations as they arise."* [156] But we are told, in the same section of the Manual, not to worry when we go through the inevitable period of relinquishment because, *"...he learns that where he anticipated grief, he finds a happy lightheartedness instead; where he thought something was asked of him, he finds a gift bestowed on him..."*

I attended a workshop in London recently by Nouk Sanchez and Tomas Vieira. It was all about undoing the ego and I found it extremely interesting. They mentioned the fact that they had been studying and teaching *ACIM* for many years but that even after a period of ten years they still got angry at times and had to work hard at practicing forgiveness. But they said that if we are serious about enlightenment, we really have to do this personal transformation work, as no one can achieve enlightenment if they cling to their ego. They are the co-authors of a really good book entitled *Take Me to Truth*, which I have read at least twice. The focus of the book is undoing the ego and in one chapter they deal with the changes that occur in us as we go through the undoing process. *"Socializing and engaging in everyday conversation often reveals a striking contrast of beliefs and values in the early stages of Undoing. We may suddenly find that because of this fundamental change we cannot be inauthentic and engage in meaningless conversation that is largely disempowering and, quite honestly, a waste of time and energy....Occasionally too, previous hobbies, interests or even passions can diminish in*

---

[154] Ibid., pp.135-136.
[155] *ACIM*, T211.
[156] *ACIM*, M10.

importance now...Anything that previously gave us a false sense of identity or security will require transformation or elimination." [157]

So it would seem that I am not alone as I go through changes in my personal life. But of course it is to be expected because when one's belief system is turned upside down, then it is bound to have an impact on one's life. Before I became an *ACIM* student I thought I had all my beliefs sorted out and I took comfort from them, but I am glad that I kept on searching for the truth and did not close my mind off to the possibility of changing my beliefs if necessary. What a pleasant surprise it was for me to find the truth in *ACIM*. I will not look back as I am convinced that the teachings of the *Course* will take me back Home, provided I practice them and don't just pay lip service to the theory part of the teachings.

In the summer of 1997, Princess Diana died a tragic death. It was a sad event, especially for her two children, but the reaction of the public to it was out of all proportion, in my opinion. She was a good woman who championed a number of important causes, but judging by the way she was mourned after her death, one would have thought she was a saint. Huge numbers of people lined the streets greatly distressed at her sudden death. Then six days later a person who had almost achieved sainthood passed away in complete destitution in another corner of the world. Mother Teresa, the Macedonian-born nun who founded the Missionaries of Charity and who had devoted her entire life to the service of the most downtrodden and deprived people of Calcutta, died of a heart attack. The media coverage for that event and the reaction of the public was minimal when compared to the coverage of the death of Princess Diana. At the time that struck me as odd. The way the people were wailing in the streets of London, one would have thought that a saint had passed away. But people were mourning for a young, beautiful, glamorous and wealthy woman. Is that indicative of the fact that our values are upside down and topsy turvy? I think it is.

The trouble is we have selected own role models based on the things we have now come to value. And as we value, above all else, material wealth, beauty, glamour and anything that improves our physical appearance and comfort, our role models will of course reflect these choices. We do not have a proper guide to

---

[157] Nouk Sanchez & Tomas Vieira, *Take me to Truth*, pp. 106-208, O Books, Hants, UK, 2007.

lead us out of the abyss that the ego has placed us in, and so in that respect we are not really to blame. It is never useful to feel guilty. All we need do is to recognise that we were looking for meaning in all the wrong places and then decide to choose wisely. For those who follow the teachings of *ACIM*, the Holy Spirit is the Guide Who will lead us Home. There are other guides, I am sure.

Gnosticism, which prevailed in the 1st to 3rd centuries AD (and possibly before Christianity), propounded an interesting theory of creation. Sophia, a feminine creative force, was deemed to be the Spirit of God. She produced a child who was later called the Demiurge and considered to be flawed and different from his mother. The Demiurge had his own creative powers and he produced the physical world. The Gnostics believed that human beings are divine spirits trapped in this physical world that was created without the permission of God. I would like to speculate and suggest that this Demiurge could in fact be the ego. According to *ACIM*, the ego, very different from God but still possessing some creative powers of its own, produced the world of matter and of multiplicity. Human beings are trapped in the world of the ego until they are able to free themselves and return to their original form (spirit) in their original home (Heaven.) Well, that is just speculation but I do see a similarity between the Demiurge and the ego.

The philosopher, psychologist and mystic, Ken Wilber, has put forward a theory of creation that is similar to *ACIM*. In his book *The Spectrum of Consciousness* he states the view that in reality there is nothing but Mind, which is limitless and beyond time and space. However, because of *maya*, a dualistic world appears—a world of unreal dualities or divisions. The problem is that, "*...man behaves in every way as if they were real; and being thus duped, man clings to his first and primordial dualism, that of subject vs. object, self vs. not-self....*" [158] He also deals with the topic of projection, which we come across quite frequently in the *Course*, and says, "*This underlying unity now appears or manifests itself or projects itself as a world of 'separate' objects extended in space and time...Dualism-Repression-Projection: this is the threefold process of maya...*" [159] Further on in his most

---

[158] Ken Wilber, *The Spectrum of Consciousness*, p. 106, Quest Books, The Theosophical Publishing House, Illinois, USA, 1985, www.questbooks.net.

[159] Ibid., p.118

interesting book, on page 142, Ken Wilber then discusses the idea of projection by the ego and explains, "*...the individual splits off facets of his own psyche, facets which he now perceives as existing external to him, usually in other people. The individual correctly perceives these facets, ideas, emotions, drives, qualities and other messages, but his meta-communicative processes incorrectly identify the source of the messages, so that the individual disowns or alienates aspects of himself and then projects or appears to perceive them in the environment.*" He then says that this process leaves the individual with a very poor self-image and can lead to neuroses.

This is where I see a strong similarity with the teachings of *ACIM*, which state that the ego projects all its original fear and guilt (which stem from the separation from God at the time of the splitting of the mind) onto others. The ego is therefore judgemental, vengeful and unforgiving. Lesson 22 of the Workbook states, "*Having projected his anger onto the world, he sees vengeance about to strike at him. His own attack is thus perceived as self defence. This becomes an increasingly vicious circle until he is willing to change how he sees. Otherwise, thoughts of attack and counter-attack will preoccupy him and people his entire world. What peace of mind is possible to him then?*" And in the Text the reason for projection is explained in this way: "*This brother who stands beside you still seems to be a stranger. You do not know him, and your interpretation of him is very fearful. And you attack him still, to keep what seems to be yourself unharmed* (this is the purpose of projection.) *Yet in his hands is your salvation. You see his madness, which you hate because you share it....*" [160]

Looking around me I can now detect numerous examples of projection. When the global financial crisis struck, a number of countries pointed their fingers at other countries and said they were to blame for causing the crisis. Similarly whenever one country is taken to task over global warming for instance, it inevitably tries to shift the blame elsewhere. And at my place of work, in the classroom, I see projection almost every day. If a teacher reprimands a pupil for talking in class, his immediate reaction will be, "*It's not just me that's talking. Look at Joe.*" Similarly if ever a child is told off for swearing his reaction will be, "*Everybody does it!*" These are just a few examples of the ego's tactic of projection. If one is observant one will notice that it happens all the time. This is because the

---

[160] *ACIM*, T422.

ego projects its feelings of guilt and inadequacy onto others, to make it feel better about itself. Furthermore, the guilt that is experienced is actually a replay of the guilt experienced aeons ago at the time of the separation from God. Knowing this, one can make a point of not projecting in this way anymore. This entails watching oneself and biting one's tongue just before one is tempted to project something onto someone else.

Another good description of the mechanism of projection can be found in the Text on page 587. "*The world you see depicts exactly what you thought you did. Except that now you think that what you did is being done to you. The guilt for what you thought is being placed outside yourself, and on a guilty world that dreams your dreams and thinks your thoughts instead of you. It brings its vengeance, not your own....The world but demonstrates an ancient truth; you will believe that others do to you exactly what you think you did to them. But once deluded into blaming them you will not see the cause of what they do, because you want the guilt to rest on them. How childish is the petulant device to keep your innocence by pushing guilt outside yourself, but never letting go!*" And so we see how the world of the ego can only ever be a world full of conflict and chaos. No wonder there is so much aggression on our planet. It can never be otherwise until we realise that this world is just an illusion; until we choose spirit over flesh, eternity over time and life over death. The problem, of course, is how to do that. One solution can be found in the teachings of *ACIM*.

Theosophy is another belief system that has some basic tenets that are in complete agreement with the teachings of *ACIM*. Theosophists believe in the unity of mankind with God and they believe that the physical world is *not* real. Helena Blavatsky (1831–1891), the founder of the Theosophical Society, was a great thinker and a prolific writer. Her books focused on esoteric spiritual knowledge known as the Ageless Wisdom, which underlies religion, science and philosophy. In one of her books, *The Key to Theosophy*, she explained that no one creates the universe but, "*Occultists and Theosophists, see in it the only universal and eternal reality casting a periodical reflection of itself on the infinite Spatial depths. This reflection, which you regard as the objective material universe, we consider as a temporary illusion and nothing else. That alone which is eternal is real."* [161] The reference in this passage to *"periodical reflection"* refers to the belief that the universe appears on the plane of objectivity or of physical manifestation every so often and, in a cyclical fashion, it constantly appears and then disappears over very long periods of time. It is interesting to note that, *"That alone which is eternal is real,"* is exactly the same teaching as *ACIM*. *"The world you see is an illusion of a world. God did not create it, for what He creates must be eternal as Himself. Yet there is nothing in the world you see that will endure forever."* [162]

I came across an interesting discussion about illusion on the Internet, in an e-book entitled *The Conquest of Illusion*, by the Dutch Theosophist J.J. van der Leeuw. The website is the spiritual and religious information website of Katinka Hesselink. In the book the author explained that it is not strictly accurate to state that physical objects are illusions and he pointed out that, *"The physical world in itself, the chair and the table in themselves, the stone or the tree in itself, are one and all as real as I am myself. But what I usually call the table, the chair, the stone or the tree is the image produced in my consciousness by the table, chair, stone or tree as it exists in the world of the Real. These images are only relatively real, that is to say they are real for me, in so far as they are my interpretation of the thing in itself...It is when I begin to look upon this image in my consciousness as an outside reality, and identify it with the thing in itself, that illusion enters...There is a world of Reality...That world is Life or Truth, or whatever else we may call ultimate Reality; that world is the Absolute, for there is all that is or was or shall be. In that world there is interaction between the different creatures and objects and as a result of that interaction every creature becomes aware in his consciousness of a world-image, the shadow cast by reality. Since, however, that shadow play is all we normally know of the real world, we identify it with that real world and look upon it as a reality independent of our consciousness and standing outside us. That is the great Illusion."* [163]

So here we see that physical objects are deemed to be reflections or images of

---

[161] H P. Blavatsky, *The Key to Theosophy*, Section 6, *The Unity of All in All*, The Theosophical Society, Pasadena, California, www.theosociety.org/pasadena/key/key-6.htm.

[162] *ACIM, Clarification of Terms, p. 85.*

[163] J. J. van der Leeuw LL.D, *The Conquest of Illusion*, Chapter 2, From the Unreal to the Real, www.katinkahesselink.net/other/conquest2.html.

the real world and our task then is to awaken from the world of illusion and return to reality. *"If it is true that our world-image is indeed an image produced in the cave of our consciousness by a reality beyond, it is evidently our first task, to thread, not merely in thought but in reality, the path leading to the world of the Real."* J.J. van der Leeuw also said that the physical body is just as much an image produced in our consciousness by an unknown reality as is any other object. Therefore, we should not identify with the body.

Finally, I would like to end this chapter with this rather humorous quotation by Wei Wu Wei: *"If a person wishes to make a study of illusion, in spite of the fact that his own body is an illusion, we are reduced to the absurdity of an illusion studying an illusion."* [164]

---

[164] Wei Wu Wei, *Fingers Pointing towards the Moon*, p. 64-65, First Sentient Publications, Colorado, USA, 2003.

Chapter 5

The One Mind

"Be conscious of your oneness with God—conscious that God is the Mind of the individual, whether that individual is you or someone else you have in thought." [165]

It can be quite difficult to believe that our minds are joined to God's. In fact, many people would find it really hard to accept this idea. Yet before the separation from God when the mind split, we were all joined together at the level of spirit/mind. But the *Course* explains, *"It is difficult for anyone who thinks he is in this world to believe this of himself. Yet the reason he thinks he is in this world is because he does not believe it."* [166]

So why do we believe that we are not part of God's mind? Because when the mind split in two, the "wrong" portion of the mind, which created (miscreated) the ego, suffered from amnesia and forgot all about its true origins. *"The Garden of Eden, or the pre-separation condition, was the state of mind in which nothing was needed. When Adam listened to the 'lies of the serpent,' all he heard was untruth. You do not have to continue to believe what is not true unless you choose to do so. All that can literally disappear in the twinkling of an eye because it is merely a misperception. What is seen in dreams seems to be very real. Yet the Bible says that a deep sleep fell upon Adam,*

---

[165] Joel S Goldsmith, *Spiritual Interpretation of Scripture,* p. 40, Willing Publishing Company, San Gabriel, California, 1969.

[166] *ACIM,* W53.

and nowhere is there reference to his waking up. The world has not yet experienced any comprehensive reawakening or rebirth. Such a rebirth is impossible as long as you continue to project or miscreate. It still remains within you, however, to extend as God extended His Spirit to you." [167] So we are all still sleeping, unless we decide to use our bodies as "learning devices" so as to change our perceptions about the world of phenomena and attempt to find out about the world of reality.

I would like to comment on two words mentioned in the previous passage: *project* and *extend*. In fact, one of the basic teachings of the *Course* is that human beings can only really do two things. They either project thoughts, emotions, beliefs, etc., that are within them (and this is usually something that emanates from the ego) or they can extend from themselves to others, as God does to them. Extension in the *Course* refers to extending love and forgiveness. When you extend love and forgiveness it is not possible at the same time to project any negative emotions, fear or guilt. It is therefore one of the ways of overcoming the dominance of the ego.

Well, to return to the concept of the One Mind, the Bodhidharma, whom I spoke about in Chapter 2, explained, *"Our nature is the mind. And the mind is our nature. This nature is the same as the mind of all buddhas....But deluded people don't realize that their own mind is the Buddha. They keep searching outside...."* [168] and the Bodhidharma said that the mind is basically pure. This corresponds with the statement above, *"My mind is part of God's. I am very holy."*

Huang Po also taught about the concept of the One Mind. Translating an ancient Chinese text into English is no mean feat, but John Blofeld did an admirable job in explaining some of the more difficult metaphysical concepts used by Huang Po in his book *The Zen Teaching of Huang Po*. In a footnote that deals with the doctrine of *Anatman* or non-self he explained that Theravada Buddhists denied man had an ego and also denied the concept of the One Mind; however, he said that the Mahayana Buddhists embrace the concept of the One Mind and believe that the ego or *Anatman* or non-self is part of the One Mind. As for Zen adepts, like the Mahayana Buddhists, they, *"take Anatman to imply 'no*

[167] *ACIM*, T17 & 18.

[168] Red Pine, *The Zen Teaching of Bodhidharma*, p. 25, North Point Press, New York, 1989.

entity to be termed an ego, naught but the One Mind, which comprises all things and gives them their only reality.' [169] However, I have noticed that some of the Buddhist teachers I have spoken to do, in fact, *deny* the existence of the concept of the One Mind.

In the same book, on page 29, there is a sermon recorded by P'eu Hsiu that reads, *"The Master said to me: All the Buddhas and all sentient beings are nothing but the One Mind, beside which nothing exists. This Mind, which is without beginning, is unborn and indestructible...."*

It is not surprising that some Buddhist teachings include the concept of the One Mind because the belief that we are all part of One Mind (or the Absolute or God) is the basic premise of non-dualism, although Buddhists do not believe that the One Mind is equivalent to God.   In *A Disappearance of the Universe* the Ascended Master Arten explains the concept of pure non-dualism to Gary Renard like this: *"...it says anything that comes from God must be exactly like Him. God could not create anything that is not perfect or else He wouldn't be perfect. The logic of that is flawless. If God is perfect and eternal, then by definition anything He creates would also have to be perfect and eternal."* [170] I think it is therefore quite evident that God could not have created our human bodies as the words "perfect" and "eternal" could hardly be used to describe them.   But if we remember also that *ACIM* says that we are "extensions" of God, then being perfect and eternal *and being extensions too* would make us all part of the One Mind, which includes God. I wonder if the emphasis on *inclusion* in modern society today stems from this belief, even if only at the subconscious level.

The following passage in *ACIM* reiterates the concept of the One Mind: *"Cause and effect are one, not separate. God wills you learn what always has been true: that He created you as part of Him, and this must still be true because ideas leave not their source."* [171] God created all of us (spirits not bodies) as part of Him, and therefore we are all equal and we must also be holy. As we can see from Lesson

---

[169] John Blofeld, *The Zen Teaching of Huang Po,* p. 110 footnote, © 1958 by John Blofeld. Used by permission of Grove/Atlantic, Inc. & by the Society of Authors on behalf of the Buddhist Society, www.societyofauthors.org.

[170] Gary Renard, *The Disappearance of the Universe,* p. 39, Hay House Inc., Carlsbad, CA, 2004.

[171] *ACIM,* T556.

299 in the Workbook, *"Eternal holiness abides in me"*; and Lesson 40 tells us, *"I am blessed as a Son of God."* I would like to digress for a moment and point out that we are all considered to be Sons of God in *ACIM* because we are all created by God. However, Jesus holds a special place as he overcame the ego and became enlightened long ago and from then on he has taken up the role of "God's Helper" in the terminology of *ACIM*. (We are told that there are other Helpers.) Being the author of *ACIM*, we can see that Jesus seems to be very keen on awakening all of humanity so that we become like Him and are able to return Home. What a wonderful service to humanity he is performing! It should also be remembered that Jesus called the Holy Spirit down upon the earth to be the Voice for God and to mediate between the ego and the spirit.

Lesson 183 in the Workbook teaches us, *"I call upon God's Name and on my own"*, and explains, *"God's Name is holy, but no holier than yours. To call upon His Name is but to call upon your own.... Your Father's Name reminds you who you are, even within a world that does not know; even though you have not remembered it."* This implies that we know that we are one with God but have forgotten it. I can well imagine that this idea is completely rejected by the followers of some orthodox religions, which tend to emphasise sin and guilt. Yet one of the goals of the teachings of *ACIM* is to help us remember who we are. Do we want to cover up the truth or do we want to discover or remember it?

We come across the concept of holiness or purity in Jnana Yoga. Swami Vivekananda pointed out that the reason why everyone seems to be searching for God or for a perfect ideal is because we are all one with God. *"It is the God within your own self that is propelling you to seek for Him, to realise Him....He for whom you have been seeking all over the world... is your own Self, the reality of your life, body, and soul. That is your own nature. Assert it, manifest it. Not to become pure, you are pure already. You are not to be perfect, you are that already."* [172] Vivekananda wrote in detail, in the chapter on the real nature of man, about the fact that the Infinite is man's true nature and he stressed that things of the senses will never bring us happiness because true happiness can only be found in the Spirit.

The concept of the One Mind is very clearly stated in the Hindu scripture, the

---

[172] Swami Vivekananda, *Jnana Yoga*, p. 37, Advaita Ashrama, Calcutta, 1993.

Bhagavad Gita. In Chapter 13, verse 16, Krishna speaks about Brahman or God and says, *"He is ONE in all, but it seems as if he were many...."* and in verse 28 we read, *"And when a man sees that the God in himself is the same God in all that is, he hurts not himself by hurting others: then he goes indeed to the Highest Path."* [173] Not only do we see the same emphasis on the unity of all creation as we do in *ACIM*, but we also see that hurting others is deemed to be hurting oneself, which is exactly what the *Course* teaches. It also says that when we forgive others we are actually forgiving ourselves too. Similarly, when we judge others we are judging ourselves. *"Look once again upon your brother, not without the understanding that he is the way to Heaven or to hell, as you perceive him. But forget not this; the role you give to him is given you, and you will walk the way you pointed out to him because it is your judgement on yourself."* [174] Our brothers (i.e., all other people) can either take us to Heaven if we practice the teachings of the *Course* and are always loving and forgiving towards them; or they can keep us trapped here on earth (hell) if we are *not* able to follow the instructions of the *Course* and are therefore aggressive towards them, or revengeful, unforgiving or judgemental about them.

"One Soul abides in all. There is one humanity. There is one brotherhood. There is one Atmahood (soul.) None is high. None is low. All are equal...When one Atman dwells in all living beings, then why do you hate others?" [175] So said the Indian sage Swami Sivananda, and although some of his teachings do not conform with those of *ACIM*, when it comes to the concept of the unity of all of creation, there is indeed a similarity. Swami Sivananda asked why all the peoples of the world cannot live in peace. He advised his disciples to repeat affirmations such as, *"I am the all; I am in all; I am the immortal Self in all."* These affirmations, he said, would help them become aware of their divine spiritual nature and would help lead them to self-perfection. Although he didn't focus on forgiveness as much as the *Course* does, in his book *Bliss Divine*, he gave the following advice, *"Do not cause pain or suffering to any living being from greed, selfishness, irritability or annoyance. Give up*

---

[173] Juan Mascaro, *The Bhagavad Gita,* Chapter 13, verses 16 & 28, pp. 100-101, Penguin Books, 1988.

[174] *ACIM*, T529.

[175] Swami Sivananda, *Bliss Divine – A Book of Spiritual Essays on the Lofty Purpose of Human Life and the Means to its Achievement,* p. 22 compiled by Sri Ananthanarayanan, The Divine Life Society, Himalayas, India, 2006.

anger or ill-will. Give up the spirit of fighting. Try your level best to keep a serene mind always."   And here we can see that he is talking about the ego's traits and the need to overcome them. He is also speaking about the doctrine of ahimsa or non-violence, which is a very important component of Hinduism. We can make a comparison with the teachings of the *Course* because if you stop to think about it, forgiveness is a definite feature of non-violence. If all of us were forgiving we would cause no pain or suffering to each other and there would be no wars.

"We live in succession, in division, in parts, in particles. Meantime within man is the soul of the whole; the wise silence; the universal beauty, to which every part and particle is equally related; the eternal ONE." [176] Those were the words of the eminent philosopher, thinker, poet and essayist, Ralph Waldo Emerson (1803–1882), who was one of America's best known 19th Century figures. He believed in non-dualism and studied, among other things, the Vedas and the Bhagavad Gita. In his essay the "Over-Soul" he said that the One Mind or the "eternal One", as he called it, was responsible for the seer and the spectacle or the subject and the object being one and the same thing.

I mentioned Theosophy in the previous chapter, but I feel that it is important to note to what extent theosophists emphasise the unity of all of creation, as this is one of their most fundamental beliefs. The website of the Theosophical Society in Pasadena, California is a mine of information and I think this quote is particularly relevant when discussing the topic of the One Mind. *"A primary idea is the essential oneness of all beings. Life is everywhere throughout the cosmos because all originates from the same unknowable divine source. Consequently, everything from the subatomic to plants, animals, humans, planets, stars, and galaxies is alive and evolving. Each is divine at its root and expresses itself through spiritual, intellectual, psychological, ethereal, and material ranges of consciousness and substance. Evolution reflects this emerging self-expression of faculties which differentiates into material forms; develops spiritual and conscious aspects; and, over cosmic time-periods, returns to the divine source. The life of the individual, of humanity, and of the entire earth is part of this*

---

[176] Ralph Waldo Emerson, *Self-Reliance and Other Essays,* p. 52, Chapter on The Over-Soul, Dover Publications Inc., New York, 1993.

cosmic process." [177] Although in this passage we see less of an emphasis on the illusory nature of the world of phenomena than we did in the last chapter, we can still see how theosophists believe that we are all united with each other and, because of our divine source, we are also united with God. I should point out though that *ACIM* does not share the belief that all forms of life in the physical universe are evolving, rather we are "awakening" from the illusion of separation and although we are progressing towards Heaven, we never actually left it in the first place. So, in the teachings of the *Course*, there is no real place for the concept of spiritual evolution although *within the illusion* we do need to evolve and become better human beings able to practice forgiveness at all times.

However, there is a further analogy that can be made between Theosophy and *ACIM*. On the same web page we see why compassion follows from the idea of the One Mind: *"Exhibiting this fundamental oneness, altruism and compassion are human expressions of cosmic and planetary realities. Humanity is more closely joined inwardly than physically, and our thoughts and feelings have a potent impact on others. By following our highest inner promptings as best we can, we benefit our immediate surroundings and humanity as a whole. The ideal is to put the welfare of humanity and all that lives ahead of one's own progress."* That is a most beautiful passage and *compassion* mentioned here could be compared with *forgiveness* in *ACIM*, although the latter teaches us that if we forgive others we actually benefit ourselves as well, so that our spiritual progress, or rather our awakening, is enhanced by being forgiving.

A very clear message in *ACIM* is that we are all One, appearing as many. So many passages refer to the fact that there is no difference between any of us. Furthermore, there is no difference between us and Christ. We are all Sons of God. It is, in fact, one of the most "inclusive" books I have ever read. If there is no difference between you and me that means that all the petty, ridiculous boundaries that we have set up to segregate ourselves from each other are totally without foundation. I am referring to differences of gender, nationality, religion, race, sexuality, class, financial status, etc. They are just not real because all the

---

[177] The Theosophical Society, Pasadena, California, *Some Basic Concepts of Theosophy*, www.theosociety.org.

millions of us on this planet, when we awaken from the dream, will return Home and find that we are all joined together in perfect harmony. Wow! But it takes a big stretch of the imagination to visualise this concept, given the complete mess we have made of our planet and our inter-relationships at all levels, local, national and international.

"Behold your role within the universe! To every part of true creation has the Lord of Love and life entrusted all salvation from the misery of hell. And to each one has He allowed the grace to be a savior to the holy ones especially entrusted to his care. And this he learns when first he looks upon one brother as he looks upon himself, and sees the mirror of himself in him... And in this single vision does he see the face of Christ, and understands he looks on everyone as he beholds this one...." [178] So we are reflections of each other and reflections of Christ.

I would like to add one more short paragraph because it resonates strongly with me: *"As beings rooted in divinity, we each have the ability to discover reality for ourselves. To do this we must learn to judge what is true and false, real and illusory; not blindly follow the dictates of authority, however high."* [179] This resonates strongly with me because it spells out exactly what I have been trying to do for the last 25 years of my life. I believe all spiritual seekers would agree with the fact that they have to judge for themselves what is true and what is false. And so many of us these days refuse to follow the dictates of authority, preferring instead to have the freedom to find and follow our own belief systems. The reason why *ACIM* is such a blessing, in my opinion, is because it has the aim of leading us from the unreal to the real. All three parts of the *Course*, the Text, Workbook and Manual, are concerned with trying to correct our false perceptions of the world and of ourselves and replacing them with the Truth.

---

[178] *ACIM*, T664.

[179] The Theosophical Society, Pasadena, California, *Some Basic Concepts of Theosophy*, www.theosociety.org.

Chapter 6

Trapped in Time

"Memory may be regarded as the cement of the ego." [180]

Many years ago I put the following thoughts down on paper. It wasn't that I was feeling particularly pessimistic about life; it was just something I had observed by looking at my own life.

FOR EVERY PLUS IN LIFE THERE HAS TO BE A MINUS

For every plus in life, there has to be a minus,

For every happy moment, a moment of sadness.

For every bit of laughter, there'll be some tears,

For every hope, you'll have some fears.

For every sunshine, there'll be some rain,

For every good feeling, there'll be some pain.

For every bit of good, there has to be bad,

For every happy memory, a memory so sad.

---

[180] Wei Wu Wei *Fingers Pointing towards the Moon*, p. 47, First Sentient Publications, Colorado, USA, 2003.

For every hot passion, only cold at the end,

For every single birth, there has to be a death.

But what is saddest of all in my mind

Is that for every 'hello', you have to say `goodbye'.

As long as we go on searching for happy moments, laughter, sunshine, passion, etc., in this world of ours, we will be unable to avoid the sad moments too. Because this is just the way things are in the world of the ego, the world of yin and yang, of duality and transient pleasures. And that was what Buddha suddenly discovered one day sitting under the Bodhi tree.

"It is impossible to seek for pleasure in the body and not find pain. It is essential that this relationship be understood, for it is one the ego sees as proof of sin. It is not really punitive at all. It is but the inevitable result of equating yourself with the body, which is the invitation to pain." [181] The word "sin" refers to the ego's perception of itself. It thinks it has sinned because of the initial separation from God and the "escape" into the world of form. The *Course* explains, in the same paragraph, that because of our guilt, we feel fearful and, *"....whatever fear directs the body to do is therefore painful. It will share the pain of all illusions, and the illusion of pleasure will be the same as pain."*

It was the surprising discovery that the illusion of pleasure is the same as the illusion of pain that spurred me on in my quest for the Truth. There is nothing wrong with seeking happiness on earth, but if we do it to the exclusion of all else and don't try to find a purpose to life, we will be stuck in the world of *samsara* or phenomena, living, dying and reincarnating, living, dying and reincarnating, etc., etc. I have finally had enough and have decided that there is no more time to waste; I *must find a way out of this illusory world*. It's not that I have had an unhappy life, because I haven't. I have so many happy memories and have been to so many wonderful places. It's just that happy memories, wonderful places, good times, etc. are no longer enough for me. My goal is to awaken from the dream and achieve liberation from the world of form. It may take me several

---

[181] *ACIM*, T415.

more lifetimes but I will persist. What is heartening is that more and more people now feel the same way. A growing number of us are determined to set ourselves free. One need but look at all the websites that offer guidance and advice on personal transformation and spiritual evolution, and all the books that are being written on this topic, to realise that this is a fact.

I must admit that it is easier for me to decide to "wake up" now than it would have been ten years ago. I am older now and no longer ruled by my hormones. But even five years ago, if I had been introduced to *A Course in Miracles* I am not sure if I would have been completely ready to follow its teachings. Thankfully at this point in my life, I am. However, I quite understand that some of the readers of this book may not be ready to take all the teachings of *ACIM* on board. And that's OK. I think the seeds will have been sown and maybe, later on in life, they may pick up *ACIM* and think, *"Now is the right time for me."* I am well aware that other readers may consider the teachings to be of little value to them and just walk away. And that's OK too. There are many Paths back Home. What is important for a disciple (and all us of seekers are disciples) is that he selects the Path that feels right to him.

I have been wearing blinkers for so long and, as I look around me at all the people rushing around so busy in their daily lives, I can't help thinking that the vast majority of us have been doing the same. Our daily lives consist of waking up, going to work, doing the household chores, watching television or reading a book, perhaps taking some form of exercise, maybe going out with friends and then going to sleep at night. And this goes on, day after day, month after month, year after year and lifetime after lifetime. How many really stop and think about the meaning of life? Or should I say the meaninglessness of life? Sometime I feel like a hamster trapped in a cage, running around and around on a little wheel just to pass the time of day. Only my little wheel is the wheel of fortune or the karmic wheel of life, bringing me pleasure and pain and more of the same. No more — the time has finally come for me to take a positive stand and jump off that karmic wheel that has been rotating incessantly for aeons and aeons.

But why do I feel "trapped"? I think it is because I am; we all are trapped in time and as long as we live in this world of illusions, we will remain that way. There's no means of escaping from the alternating cycles of life and death and death and life *unless one awakens from the dream.*

Time is the most fascinating, baffling and mind-boggling topic that is dealt with in *ACIM*. We are all so used to thinking of it in linear terms with the present following on from the past and the future following on from the present, but in reality time is just not like that. The *Course* teaches us that far from being linear, time is holographic, i.e., every present moment contains all other moments. Thus the past, present and future are all taking place *simultaneously,* only we choose to focus on one segment of it at any given time. Time is one of the major illusions that was created by the ego at the time of the separation. The split mind devised space, time and the world of phenomena to "escape" from Heaven and we have been trapped in all this ever since.

In one of my favourite movies, *Groundhog Day,* a grumpy weatherman awakens one morning and the next and then the next, to discover that he is living the same day over and over again until he becomes a reformed character and is able to free himself from the trap—the trap of time. An analogy can be made here between the weatherman and us human beings because we are really living lifetime after lifetime in the same way that the weatherman in the film lived through one particular day repeatedly. We have no way of escaping from the illusion of time until we awaken from the dream.

The reason we are trapped in time is explained very clearly in *ACIM: "Each day, and every minute in each day, and every instant that each minute holds, you but relive the single instant when the time of terror took the place of love. And so you die each day to live again, until you cross the gap between the past and present, which is not a gap at all. Such is each life; a seeming interval from birth to death and on to life again, a repetition of an instant gone by long ago that cannot be relived. And all of time is but the mad belief that what is over is still here and now."* [182] This profound passage needs an explanation. The time of terror referred to here, is the time of separation when the mind split and created the ego. Thus we (the wrong portion of the mind) entered the world of the ego, a world of manifest objects and of time and space. But we are told that the gap between the past and present doesn't really exist; thus time is an illusion and therefore it cannot be relived. The moment of

---

[182] *ACIM,* T552.

separation is referred to as a *"tiny tick of time"* that ended as soon as it started and didn't really take place at all (I did say this was a baffling topic) but the ego believes that it did take place and that time is not an illusion.

"Time lasted but an instant in your mind, with no effect upon eternity. And so is all time past, and everything exactly as it was before the way to nothingness was made. The tiny tick of time in which the first mistake (the separation) *was made, and all of them within that one mistake, held the Correction for that one, and all of them that came within the first."* Time had no effect upon eternity because the separation didn't really happen. The Correction mentioned here is the Holy Spirit. *"To you who still believe you live in time and know not it is gone, the Holy Spirit still guides you through the infinitely small and senseless maze you still perceive in time, though it has long since gone."* [183] In the *Course* time is considered to be but a little hindrance to eternity but, because we believe in it, we can put it to good use by living under the direction of the Holy Spirit, as He represents the "right" portion of the mind. We do this by turning to Him for advice and asking Him for guidance whenever we are unsure what to do or how to react to a particular situation. This is called the holy instant in the *Course*.

> *This holy instant would I give to You.*
>
> *Be You in charge. For I would follow You,*
>
> *Certain that Your direction gives me peace.*[184]

I have made up a little tune to those few lines and I sing them every day. If we really do follow the instructions of the Holy Spirit all the time (and it takes a great deal of hard work to do this and to *remember* to do this consistently), we will be well rewarded. *"Can you imagine what it means to have no cares, no worries, no anxieties, but merely to be perfectly calm and quiet all the time? Yet that is what time is for; to learn just that and nothing more."* [185]

If we let ourselves be guided by the Holy Spirit, we will learn how to forgive

---

[183] *ACIM*, T550.
[184] *ACIM*, W486, Lessons 361 to 365.
[185] *ACIM*, T301.

and this is the key to eternity. *"Forgiveness is the great release from time. It is the key to learning that the past is over....The unforgiven is a voice that calls from out a past forevermore gone by. And everything that points to it as real is but a wish that what is gone could be made real again and seen as here and now, in place of what is really now and here...And do you want that fearful instant kept, when Heaven seemed to disappear and God was feared and made a symbol of your hate?"* [186] In other words, the ego clings to the moment of separation because by doing that it is clinging onto its own existence. It therefore wants to relive that moment (the fearful instant) over and over again and so it *wants* to remain trapped in time. The question is: do we want to remain trapped in time?

How exactly does the ego keep us trapped in time? By making sure a steady stream of memories flits across our minds—both sad and happy memories—and by keeping us hooked on the future by means of planning and anticipating good things to come. I know about these so well. As I sit and watch my thoughts I can observe my own ego doing just this and it is most irritating.

In his well known essay, *Self-reliance,* Emerson observed that human beings do not live in the present. They either remember things from their past or they strive to peer into the future. He compared this with nature and said that flowers for example live only in the present and pay no attention to what has gone by or what is yet to come because, *"....they exist with God today....But man postpones or remembers; he does not live in the present, but with reverted eye laments the past, or heedless of the riches that surround him, stands on tiptoe to foresee the future."* [187] And Emerson said we will not find happiness until we can learn to live in the present, as nature does.

I would like to return to the *holy instant* because it is a crucial part of the *Course's* teachings. The holy instant can only be experienced if we are living in the present, as the present is the only moment in which we can escape from the clutches of the ego. We are told that the holy instant works *instantaneously* provided one releases the past and does not plan to apply the concept in the

---

[186] *ACIM*, T551.

[187] Ralph Waldo Emerson, *Self-Reliance and Other Essays,* p. 28, Chapter on The Self-Reliance, Dover Publications Inc., New York, 1993.

future. *"At no single instant does the body exist at all. It is always remembered or anticipated, but never experienced just **now**. Only its past and future make it seem real. Time controls it entirely, for sin (i.e., error) is never wholly in the present...It is impossible to accept the holy instant without reservation unless, just for an instant, you are willing to see no past or future."* [188]

One summer I went away to the New Forest for a few days to recharge my batteries. As I was sitting under a tree at the top of a small hill overlooking a vast undulating, panoramic landscape of awe-inspiring open heath alternating with beautiful forests, I called upon the Holy Spirit. *"I am here,"* I said, *"ready to be of service. Please talk to me, please let me hear You."* Did I hear Him? No! I just sat there and gave a sigh, wondering if I would ever hear Him. But then a few moments later an idea popped into my head. It was about the "eternal now." I don't know if the idea was from the Holy Spirit or not. But it cleared up something important in my mind.

The eternal now is something we read a lot about these days, i.e., the importance of living in the present and not focusing on the past or on the future. Books have been written on the subject and I understood from them that it was an important concept, but it was only when the following idea flashed into my mind that it all made sense to me. You can only really and truly forgive if you live in the present because if you remember any grievance or offence, then you have not really forgiven the perpetrator. Well, you may have told yourself you have forgiven them but you certainly haven't forgotten what they did; otherwise you would not have had that memory. But if you refuse to hold on to any negative memories, such as when someone said or did something that upset you, then *forgiveness will follow automatically.* Because here and now, at this present moment, nothing needs to be forgiven. Take me for example; at this present moment I am sitting peacefully in front of my computer writing and there's no annoying or irritating person around to push my buttons. This means that if all past grievances are released and not allowed to be remembered or spoken about or alluded to, then there's nothing to forgive and no one who needs to be

---

[188] *ACIM*, T388 & 389.

forgiven. *"The past is over. It can touch me not."* [189]

But what if, the reader may ask, someone really annoying comes into the room right now, whilst I am peacefully sitting in front of my computer, and says something really irksome? The answer is to try to forgive immediately or as soon as possible afterwards and then, and this is the key to it all, refuse to think about the incident ever again. That means not mentioning it to anyone else, not thinking, *"Oh, what a jerk!"* and overlooking it on the spot. I know this sounds far easier than it actually is, especially for me, as I tend to forgive but not to forget very quickly. Yet if this strategy helps you to forgive *and* it keeps you focused on the present moment, then it must certainly be an effective weapon against the ego. And as we are told in *ACIM, "Love holds no grievances."* [190] That's a lesson I repeat to myself quite frequently.

The example I gave was of someone who came along and was just a bit irritating, but if I really was abused either verbally or physically I know it would not be at all easy to completely put the incident out of my mind the moment that it happened. I think we have to be like a computer that has had its memory and history erased so that nothing is stored, saved or able to be re-visited in the future. After a few days of focusing on trying to do this, I have come to the realisation that it is extremely difficult to try to wipe out one's memory completely, especially for older people who have more stored there. (I think the reason why young children and animals find it so easy to remain totally focused on what they are doing and seem oblivious to what happened the previous day or the previous hour even, is that they haven't got very many memories accumulated in their minds.) What is needed to live in the present is the constant observation of the contents of one's mind and the immediate re-direction of one's thoughts to the present whenever one is aware that one has popped back mentally into a past moment. As we are told in *ACIM, "My mind is preoccupied with past thoughts.* [191] And it is explained quite bluntly that, *"No one really sees anything. He sees only his thoughts projected outward. The mind's preoccupation with the past is the cause of the misconception about time from which your seeing suffers.*

---

[189] *ACIM*, W442, Lesson 289.
[190] *ACIM*, W115, Lesson 68.
[191] *ACIM*, W13, Lesson 8.

Your mind cannot grasp the present, which is the only time there is. It therefore cannot understand time, and cannot, in fact, understand anything." Then Lesson 8 reminds us that the past is not here and so if we do dwell on it we are, of course, dwelling on illusions.

I have noticed that it is particularly difficult to live in the present constantly if you are on your own. I think it is because you are alone with your thoughts much more than if you live with others. When I am busy at work or shopping or running other errands I am focused on the present because I have to be to get the job done. However, as I live alone, I frequently find myself reminiscing about the past—about both happy and sad moments—unless I am very busy doing housework or reading or writing. When I am cooking I often turn on the radio as I know that classical music will help keep me in the present moment. I only realised the extent of my problem when I took the conscious decision to observe my own thoughts. Oh, how depressing it is! So what do I do? Each time I am aware that I am thinking about an unhappy memory, I call upon the Holy Spirit and I tell my ego to go take a hike! I say something along the lines of, *"Ego, nice try— get out of my mind! Holy Spirit, please help me conquer my ego and turn all my thoughts to right mindedness."* Then I look around me and concentrate on all the good things that are there, e.g., the view from the window, the cup of tea, the peaceful cat snoozing by my side, the roses in a vase on the table, etc. All this does help until the next memory pops up and I have to repeat the whole process again! However, I can't help thinking that merely by watching my own thoughts I am achieving something. Hopefully one day I will be able to live in the present continually and, as the saying goes, practice makes perfect. I should add that I really enjoy living alone and having a lot of quiet contemplation time at home, but it does mean that I have to be constantly vigilant.

One may wonder why one should push aside *happy* memories and I must acknowledge that I do enjoy them and sometimes deliberately go back and relive a particularly happy moment in my mind. But the problem is that both unhappy and happy memories stoke the ego because firstly, they make time appear to be real, when, in fact, it isn't, as it is only a fabrication of the ego; and secondly, all the emotions that accompany the memories are most probably, the vast majority of the time, the product of the ego. But by living in the now the ego is kept in its place.

I would like to digress for a moment and speak briefly about two topics of importance: looking ahead to the future and grieving for the loss of a loved one. I feel that there are times when looking ahead to the future may not be such a bad thing from the point of view of us earthlings. It is such a wonderful feeling to look forward to a particular happy event or holiday. And if, for example, you are stuck in a job you are not happy with and have applied for other jobs, it does give you hope when you think that you could find a new, more suitable job in the future. This doesn't mean *living* in the future but simply *looking forward to* something that could occur in the future and I don't think there is anything wrong with that, especially if it gives you hope and improves your mood. Of course from the point of view of the teachings of the *Course*, we should really be living in the eternal now, all the time. But however much of an illusion things may be, there are times when life seems rather difficult and I think it helps if one has something bright on the horizon to look forward to.

I also feel that we need to allow ourselves time to grieve when we experience the loss of a loved one, human or animal, because however much we know that life is an illusion, when someone we love dies, we will still grieve and I think we need to. When a loved one dies you can't just pretend it didn't really happen, because it seems *very real*. Therefore, we have to go through the grieving process in order to move on with our lives. I try to focus on the fact that we are all really spirits and that we will be reunited with those we love in the spirit world. That helps me a lot.

It was while I was still in the New Forest, partly jogging and partly walking in the early morning one day, that I realised something else that, to me, seemed significant. One way of completely losing track of time is to be absorbed by the beauty that is all around you. I was soaking up the fresh air, the vast open space, the wild animals, the trees and flowers and suddenly realised that my normal 25 minutes of exercise had turned into 45 minutes and I had not been aware of it. It was lovely to be liberated, even for just a moment, from my watch. I am sure that artists and musicians and other creative people are able to lose track of time when they are deeply involved in what they are doing. For me nature works wonders. So even if all the wondrous beauty of nature is a fabrication of the ego, it can be put to good use if it releases one from the hands of time, however momentarily.

Funnily enough, I have found that mathematics also helps me escape from the clutches of time. There was a time in my life when I was really short of money and, in order to make ends meet, I gave private mathematics lessons. I always found that I lost track of time when I was immersed in the subject and was trying to simplify it for a student. There's nothing like quadratic equations to help you forget the ticking of the clock! Maybe it is because the world of numbers is a totally different world from the one in which we live.

Another way of avoiding having a continuous awareness of time is not to wear a watch. I do this whenever I can, especially during weekends. I also make a point about being vague about the timing of future events, such as when exactly I plan to go on holiday or how many days till Christmas. Furthermore, I don't like knowing how old my friends are. But it is difficult trying to release yourself from being time bound when friends or family ring up and want to know exactly *when* you are doing this or *how old* such and such a person is. I guess we are all trapped in time and just don't realise it.

ACIM explains that we cannot be expected to know that we are actually living in eternity and are not trapped in time because the concept of eternity is not acknowledged by the ego/wrong mind. *"All healing is release from the past. That is why the Holy Spirit is the only Healer. He teaches that the past does not exist, a fact which belongs to the sphere of knowledge, and which therefore no one in the world can know. It would indeed be impossible to be in the world with this knowledge. For the mind that knows this unequivocally knows also it dwells in eternity, and utilizes no perception at all. It therefore does not consider where it is, because the concept 'where' does not mean anything to it. It knows that it is everywhere, just as it has everything, and forever."* [192] So if we can't be expected to know about the illusion of time, we should be really grateful to Jesus for teaching us this now. Knowing about the concept of eternity and about the fact that time is all part of the ego's illusory world, should make it easier for us to awaken from the dream. But if we didn't know, if we hadn't been told, then what hope would we have had?

---

[192] *ACIM*, T258.

Why does the ego need to clutch onto the concept of linear time? Because this guarantees its own survival. The *Course* tells us, *"'Now' has no meaning to the ego. The present merely reminds it of past hurts, and it reacts to the present as if it were the past, and although the past is over, the ego tries to preserve its image by responding as if it were present."* I think the next passage is vitally important: *"It dictates your reactions to those you meet in the present from a past reference point, obscuring their present reality. In effect, if you follow the ego's dictates you will react to your brother as though he were someone else, and this will surely prevent you from recognizing him as he is....The shadowy figures from the past are precisely what you must escape. They are not real, and have no hold over you unless you bring them with you....Unless you learn that past pain is an illusion, you are choosing a future of illusions and losing the many opportunities you could find for release in the present..."* [193] This is a point that has to be clearly understood. We all keep the past alive by discussing with others our misfortune or unpleasant things that have happened to us. I now make a conscious effort these days not to do this, but it is not easy. We seem to unwittingly carry pain around with us all the time. Just think of the average telephone call to a friend or relative. Yes, if you have good news you will share it with them of course, but very often the topics of discussion might be your or their health problems, health problems of your pets, the rising cost of living, environmental pollution, acts of aggression or other calamities seen on TV news bulletins, the dire political situation somewhere or other in the world, etc. I think that is one reason why I really don't enjoy long telephone conversations. However, one thing I do enjoy, as I mentioned before, is watching old black and white movies from the 1940s and 1950s. But I think that here again that ego of mine is back with another tactic to trap me by keeping memories of another era alive in my mind. But for the moment anyway I have no intention of not watching them. I am not ready to totally renounce all the pleasures of this illusory world even though I know that what we see in the cinema is just an illusion within a greater illusion.

Memories keep us trapped in the past and guilt ensnares us in the future. The *Course* calls guilty feelings *"preservers of time"*, since we expect people or situations to be just as they were in the past, when we meet them again in the

---

[193] *ACIM*, T246.

future. Thus guilty feelings, *"...induce fears of retaliation or abandonment, and thus ensure that the future will be like the past. This is the ego's continuity. It gives the ego a false sense of security by believing that you cannot escape from it. But you can and must."* [194]

It wasn't until I read Gary Renard's book *Your Immortal Reality* for a third time that I really understood the extent of the problem of guilt. It is explained by the Ascended Master Arten that we simply won't be able to live in the present until we overcome all unconscious guilt in our minds. *"Any attempt to remain in the now is doomed to failure without doing the work of true forgiveness. Until you've completely forgiven that which you made and projected outside of yourself, you are not forgiven in your own unconscious mind, and until you are, the cycle of birth and death cannot be broken."* [195] Arten goes on to explain that all guilt *must* be healed before we can live in the eternal now and this can only be done by forgiving the past and forgiving our concerns about the future. And because time is holographic, not linear, we *can* actually forgive ourselves for that initial moment of separation from God aeons ago. *"...there's no difference between forgiving the original separation at the time it appeared to happen, and forgiving it right now, for they are one and the same."* That seems amazing but only because we are so used to viewing time as being linear. That last passage shows that what we do in the so-called present *can* have an impact on the ancient past.

So it would seem that there is a strong link between being trapped in time and feeling guilty. Therefore the more we forgive others and ourselves the more likely we are to be able to free ourselves from guilt, overcome the ego and live in the present moment.

I have always been conscious of the passing of time and have never liked the thought of wasting time. That's why I don't like attending meetings at work where some people just seem to talk for the sake of it. Topics go round and round the table and it often takes hours to reach decisions that could have been reached in minutes. Whenever I convene meetings I am always direct and to the point and will not allow them to drag on indefinitely. So when I read the

---

[194] *ACIM,* T86.
[195] Gary Renard *Your Immortal Reality*, p. 193, Hay House Inc., Carlsbad, CA, 2006.

following passage in *ACIM* it struck a chord with me: *"Nothing is ever lost but time, which in the end is meaningless. For it is but a little hindrance to eternity, quite meaningless to the real Teacher of the world. Yet since you do believe in it, why should you waste it going nowhere, when it can be used to reach a goal as high as learning can achieve?"* [196] I don't think anybody wants to waste time going nowhere, but the problem is that not everyone is aware that they are on a journey Home and so they go nowhere unwittingly. But, as it says in the Bible, *"And I say unto you, Ask, and it shall be given you; seek, and ye shall find; knock, and it shall be opened unto you."* [197] And more and more of us are asking, seeking and knocking. And we *shall* find.

A *miracle* takes place when we change our perception from the ego's way of thinking to the Holy Spirit's way of thinking. It has a sort of magical or miraculous power to it because when we choose a miracle, the miracle can shift time. In the following fascinating passage we can see why the teachings of the *Course* will speed up the enlightenment process for us. *"The miracle minimizes the need for time...the miracle entails a sudden shift from horizontal to vertical perception. This introduces an interval from which the giver and receiver both emerge farther along in time than they would otherwise have been. The miracle thus has the unique property of abolishing time to the extent that it renders the interval of time it spans unnecessary....The miracle substitutes for learning that might have taken thousands of years."* [198] Thousands of years saved!

This next passage explains exactly how miracles save time. *"The miracle enables you to see your brother without his past, and so perceive him as born again. His errors are all past, and by perceiving him without them you are releasing him. And since his past is yours, you share in this release."* [199] By choosing the Holy Spirit's way of thinking we choose to forgive whatever another person may have done to us. So our brother's errors are all past. His past is ours because of the One Mind principle discussed in the preceding chapter. Thus the miracle frees both him and us, and we could be thousands of years closer to enlightenment—what an

---

[196] *ACIM*, T550.
[197] King James Bible, *Luke* 11:9.
[198] *ACIM*, T8.
[199] *ACIM*, T251.

uplifting thought. I should point out that, although *ACIM* tells us on page 5 of the Manual that, *"The world of time is the world of illusion,"* it speaks about the passage of time and about saving us thousands of years because for us, in our illusory world, time does exist and cannot be denied. Thus the quotation I made earlier in this chapter: *"To you who still believe you live in time and know not it is gone, the Holy Spirit still guides you..."* shows that linear time is acknowledged, but the only purpose it has is for us to practice forgiveness so that we can have, *"...no cares, no worries, no anxieties, but merely to be perfectly calm and quiet all the time."* Once we have practised all our forgiveness lessons and awaken from the dream, time will disappear and we will return to eternity (although strictly speaking this is not correct because we are already living in eternity but are unaware of it.)

One of the best books I have come across that deals with the illusion of time is Kenneth Wapnick's brilliant book, *"A Vast Illusion — Time according to A Course in Miracles."* It explains the whole concept in great detail and very clearly and I would recommend this book to all who are interested in the topic. With reference to the initial moment of separation from Heaven, when the split mind created the ego, he explains that in that very instant, *"....we believed we had attacked God and separated from Him, and then believed in fear that God was attacking us in return. This instant of terror houses our sin, guilt, and fear, underlying **all** our experiences. Every fearful and hateful thought has its origin here, while every forgiving and healing thought has its origin in this instant as well."* [200] When we do not forgive others we are stuck in the past, in the instant of separation. Kenneth Wapnick, on page 58 of his book, explains how: *"Whenever we feel any lack of forgiveness in ourselves, all that we are doing is calling forth that ancient instant, which has already been undone. It appears as if our upset is due to what another has done, here and now, but in reality it is the result of our decision, **here and now,** to continue to make real for ourselves that ancient instant of seeming separation, the original judgment against ourselves and against our Creator."* This is indeed food for thought and something worth considering every time an opportunity for forgiveness crops up in our lives. It shows quite clearly how being unforgiving keeps us trapped in time, in an ancient moment to be precise, and it seems like rather a foolish thing to do.

---

[200] Kenneth Wapnick, *A Vast Illusion – Time according to A Course in Miracles*, p. 60, Temecula, California, 2006, used by permission of the *Foundation for A Course in Miracles*.

Paul Brunton (1898–1981) has been one of my favourite authors for many years. He was a journalist, philosopher, traveller and above all a mystic, who travelled around the world in search of God. Whilst in India he visited gurus and sages and then he himself went through an enlightenment experience. He wrote several books which are all worth reading, but I would recommend in particular *The Quest of the Overself*, which he wrote in 1937. In that book he made a comment that could have been something one comes across in *ACIM*. Speaking about the fact that only the present is real, he pointed out that, *"It possesses no duration, and therefore it is the inlet to a timeless Absolute. In short, when isolated it is really an abstract idea existing within our minds. Thus we arrive at the curious position that 'being in time' means 'being in the present' and the latter in turn means 'being in timelessness, i.e., eternity."* Then he went on to explain, *"Hence we are living right here and now in the fullness of true eternal life, only we are quite unaware, quite unconscious of it. The restoration of this missing awareness would necessarily revolutionize our lives."* [201]

Brunton said that we will remain trapped in our concept of time unless we realise that our innermost self, or the *Overself* as he called it, transcends time and is eternal. On page 130 we read, *"So long as one wrongly identifies himself with the physical body, so long as he even still wrongly identifies himself with the mentality and the ego-memories, so long will he necessarily exist as a creature of time, a captive of past memories, present happenings and future hopes and fears."* The solution to this problem of being trapped in time is to realise, through introspection and analysis, that one's true self or the Overself is eternally free and, *"can never be affected by whatever belongs to time, even though the ego may continue to function* ***within*** *it."* So here we see that as egos we *are* all living in time, which we perceive to be linear time, but in reality this is not the case, because we are the Overself (or eternal spirit) and therefore we are immortal, eternal and free.

Ken Wilber, whom I mentioned in Chapter 4, deals with the concept of time being an illusion in his study of the evolution of the spectrum of consciousness. In his discussion of the Mahayana Buddhist Lankavatara Sutra, he says we use

---

[201] Paul Brunton, *The Quest of the Overself*, pp. 119-120, Rider, Random House, London, 2003
Reprinted by permission of the Paul Brunton Philosophic Foundation, www.paulbrunton.org.

memory to attempt to know the past and we then project this forward and create the future, despite the fact that there is nothing but the present moment: *"In this fashion do we conjure up, out of this moment, the fantastic illusion called 'time.' And since 'time' is just another name for space and objects (space-time-objects being a single continuum), the Lankavatara claims the entire universe of separate objects extended in space and succeeding one another in time, is actually generated by thought-memory wrongly interpreted, which 'reflects' the one Mind and thus apparently 'divides' that Mind, just as a mirror apparently creates two worlds from one."* [202] Thus memory creates the past and the projection of memory creates the future whereas in reality all that exists is the eternal now. The world of phenomena, time and space are produced by thought memory *in error* and this thought error is a reflection of the One Mind but it divides that Mind. The similarity here with the teachings of *ACIM* is quite apparent. The *Course* states that the wrong portion of the mind split away from the One Mind/God and created the world of subject and object *in error*. Wilber goes on to explain that we interpret memory wrongly because we separate subject from object, i.e., we have created the world of duality out of non-duality

"The eternal or the timeless is now and the now cannot be understood by a man who is caught in the net of time. To free thought from time demands action, but the mind is lazy, it is slothful, and therefore ever creates other hindrances." [203] Those were the words of the world renowned thinker and philosopher, Jiddu Krishnamurti (1895–1986), who spent most of his life travelling around the world, speaking about spiritual subjects. He was a strong believer in meditation and he said this was the way to experience the eternal now. He said memory prevented us from understanding reality. He also said personal growth or personal transformation was not a process that took time. But when one discovers the falsity of time and one quietens the mind, one is able to understand "what is," then transformation or regeneration, as he called it, is possible. So once again we see that time is deemed to be unreal and an impediment to spiritual growth.

---

[202] Ken Wilber, *The Spectrum of Consciousness*, p. 111, Quest Books, The Theosophical Publishing House, Illinois, USA, 1985, www.questbooks.net.

[203] J Krishnamurti *The First and Last Freedom*, p. 265, Victor Gollancz Ltd., Orion Publishing Group, 1978.

The Indian author and teacher K.R. Paramahamsa holds a similar view to that of Krishnamurti. He too stresses the importance of living in the present if one wishes to achieve enlightenment. *"When the mind stops linking to the past and the future, it becomes no-mind. If from moment to moment, one's mind dwells on what is, and drops it effortlessly at once, the mind becomes no-mind, full of purity. If consciousness ceases to be the finite mind, one is to know for certain that cyclic world-illusion no longer exists, and there is perfection."* [204]

Verse 16 of Bhagavan Ramana Maharshi's *Forty Verses on Reality* states, *"Do time and space exist apart from us? If we are the body we are affected by time and space. But are we the body? We are the same now, then, and forever."* And in the commentary on this verse, S. Cohen points out that time appears to be the creator and destroyer of all things for those who believe that they are the body. They therefore live in fear of time. But, *"The others who know themselves to be pure spirit are bodiless, timeless and spaceless; and, Bhagavan affirms, they are thus free from the hallucination of: 'We alone are.' Time and space are not."* [205]

I started this chapter with a brief quotation by Wei Wu Wei and I would like to end the chapter with the following passage in which he sums up the illusory concept of time: *"If there were no memory there would be no Past. If there were no desire or fear there would be no Future. The Present, renewed every instant, alone would remain, and it would be eternity for there could be no Time.... Have the Past and the Future any reality? ...Can there be anything but an eternal Present?"* [206]

[204] K. R. Paramahamsa, *Tat Sat*, p. 19, Total Recall Publications, Inc. Texas, 2007.

[205] Ramana Maharshi and Shankara, *Ramana, Shankara and the Forty Verses, The Essential Teachings of Advaita*, pp. 131-132, Watkins Publishing, London 2002.

[206] Wei Wu Wei, *Fingers Pointing towards the Moon*, p. 5, First Sentient Publications, Colorado, USA, 2003.

Chapter 7

Overcoming the Ego

"All troubles come to an end when the ego dies." [207]

The *Course* makes it very clear that the ego has to be vanquished if we are to stand any chance of overcoming its illusory world and achieving enlightenment. This belief is shared with both Buddhism and Hinduism. We are told in the *Course* that the ego is devious, self-serving, manipulative, fearful and deluded. The following passage illustrates precisely how cunning the ego is. *"The ego always tries to preserve conflict. It is very ingenious in devising ways that seem to diminish conflict, because it does not want you to find conflict so intolerable that you will insist on giving it up. The ego therefore tries to persuade you that **it** can free you of conflict, lest you give the ego up and free yourself."* [208]

But despite all its horrid, scheming characteristics, we are told not to be fearful of the ego. *"Do not be afraid of the ego. It depends on your mind, and as you made it by believing in it, so you can dispel it by withdrawing belief from it. Do not project the responsibility for your belief in it onto anyone else, or you will preserve the belief. When you are willing to accept sole responsibility for the ego's existence you will have laid aside all anger and all attack, because they come from an attempt to project responsibility for your own errors."* [209] This implies that we have to acknowledge that we (the 'wrong" portion of the split mind) created the ego, and then, when

---

[207] K. R. *Tat Sat,* p. 13, Total Recall Publications Inc., Texas 2007.
[208] *ACIM,* T130.
[209] *ACIM,* T131.

we have taken on the responsibility for the ego's errors of perception, we are advised to hand them over swiftly to the Holy Spirit to be undone. In this way the Holy Spirit plays a major part in undoing the ego. *"The Holy Spirit is in the part of the mind that lies between the ego and the spirit, mediating between them always in favour of the spirit."* A miracle is achieved when we turn from the perceptions of the ego to the Holy Spirit's way of thinking. This is the most important choice we can make and, it is, in fact, ultimately the only choice.

ACIM points out that the ego produces so much conflict, confusion and chaos in our lives that the only reason we would not want to overcome it, is that we are unaware of exactly how destructive it is. That is why I think it is so important to learn all about it and to realise that both the ego and the physical world are just illusions.

I think it was a strong awareness of the impermanent nature of our world that helped me to instantly recognise the Truth in the *Course's* teachings. As soon as I started studying *ACIM* I felt drawn to its message. Maybe this was because I have often pondered upon the meaning or meaninglessness of our existence. Losing a loved one highlights the impermanent nature of our lives. If one has always had a pet, as I have, then one is even more acutely conscious of how we are always ultimately deprived of all the things we love. I think this is because animals have such a short life span. Nothing is eternal. I should rephrase that. Nothing is eternal in the illusory world of the ego. But the ego tries to hide this from us by keeping us otherwise occupied. *"Eternalness is the one function the ego has tried to develop, but has systematically failed to achieve."* So it tries to keep our mind off this issue by its *"characteristic busyness with nonessentials.... Preoccupations with problems set up to be incapable of solution are favourite ego devices for impeding learning progress."* [210]

If we think about it, we will realise that every living thing on this planet has a built-in self-destruct mechanism, and we don't even question this! We think it is part of the "normal" scheme of things, a part of nature's grand design. We know no better. Who on this planet hasn't been touched by grief? Who hasn't been touched by loss? Every single living person ultimately will be. But we must

---

[210] *ACIM*, T66 & 67.

remember that, *"God did not create a meaningless world."*[211] God did not create a fearful, cruel and tragic world. God did not create our planet or any other. We cannot blame Him. He does not want us to suffer because in His eyes we are His holy Sons of God as we were when He first created Christ, who then created by extension. But the Son of God (Christ) did *not* create our physical bodies. He created us as *spirit*. (This reference to *Christ* creating us as spirit does not mean that God did not create us. One has to remember that Christ is one with God, so it might be more accurate to say that God *and* Christ created us through extension; but they created us in the form of spirit/mind and not in the form of a physical body.)

Another devious ego tactic is pain. Pain makes the body seem real. Anyone who has had a throbbing headache or severe back ache will be well aware of this. The ego creates pain in the body as yet another means of diversion away from the Holy Spirit. Pleasure is another of the ego's diversionary tactics. Just think of how you feel when you are enjoying a delicious, creamy ice cream. All you can do is focus on the pleasurable sensations that arise. The same goes for sex. Yet pleasure and pain are all part of the illusion. *"Pain compels attention, drawing it away from Him* (i.e., the Holy Spirit) *and focusing upon itself. Its purpose is the same as pleasure, for they both are means to make the body real....Pleasure and pain are equally unreal, because their purpose cannot be achieved....Sin* (an error in perception) *shifts from pain to pleasure, and again to pain. For either witness is the same, and carries but one message: "You are here, within this body, and you can be hurt. You can have pleasure too, but only at the cost of pain."* [212]

Guilt and fear are two things the ego cannot escape. As I have mentioned several times before, at the time of the splitting of the mind, the ego decided to separate from God and it created the universe as a place of refuge. But realising that it had abandoned God and believing it had defeated God, the ego has lived in fear ever since because it believed God would be angry with it for this, and would therefore punish it. It also feels guilty for having split away from its Source. *"The imagined usurping of functions not your own* (i.e., creating the physical

---

[211] *ACIM*, W23, Lesson 14.
[212] *ACIM*, T579 & 580.

world) *is the basis of fear. The whole world you see reflects the illusion that you have done so, making fear inevitable. To return the function to the One to Whom it belongs is thus the escape from fear. And it is this that lets the memory of love return to you."* [213] Thus following the guidance of the Holy Spirit, Who is the Voice for God, will eradicate the subconscious fear and guilt from which we all suffer.

The problem with guilt, as I have pointed out before, is that we try to avoid it by projecting it onto others. This is another cunning ego ploy to make us feel better. But it doesn't work. *"In any union with a brother in which you seek to lay your guilt upon him, or share it with him or perceive his own, **you** will feel guilty....It is inevitable that those who suffer guilt will attempt to displace it, because they do believe in it"* [214].

To summarise, the ego has an arsenal of weapons with which to keep us trapped in the illusion: time, pain, pleasure, guilt and being excessively busy. So what can we do about it? Firstly, I think it is important to be well aware of just how desperate the ego is to keep us trapped so as to ensure its own existence. *"Do not underestimate the intensity of the ego's drive for vengeance on the past. It is completely savage and completely insane. For the ego remembers everything you have done that has offended it, and seeks retribution of you....Yet without your alliance in your own destruction, the ego could not hold you to the past."* [215]

Secondly, we have to work hard to release ourselves from its clutches. One way is not to hang onto negative memories of things that happened in the past that upset us. *"Imagine slights, remembered pain, past disappointments, perceived injustices and deprivations all enter into the special relationship, which becomes a way in which you seek to restore your wounded self-esteem."* [216] So we have to let go of all the things that have upset us or offended us or harmed us and choose the "holy instant" instead. This means turning over any negative memories or thoughts or feelings to the Holy Spirit and asking Him for guidance and help in dealing with these troublesome thoughts. The holy instant is actually a tool that helps us live

---

[213] *ACIM*, M70.
[214] *ACIM*, T263.
[215] *ACIM*, T348.
[216] *ACIM*, T347 & 348.

in the present and let go of the past. *"In the holy instant it is understood that the past is gone, and with its passing the drive for vengeance has been uprooted and has disappeared."* [217] And with that comes peace of mind. I have tried it and it *has* helped, but it takes a lot of practice and sometimes I *forget* to turn every unpleasant feeling, thought or memory over to the Holy Spirit. But I hope the time will come when I can turn any unwelcome memory or thought or feeling over to the Him automatically and instantly.

Another means of overcoming the ego is to refuse to feel guilty. *"Release from guilt is the ego's whole undoing. Make no one fearful, for his guilt is yours, and by obeying the ego's harsh commandments you bring its condemnation on yourself, and you will not escape the punishment it offers those who obey it."* [218] I think I should point out that release from guilt does not mean that we go out and commit a terrible deed without feeling any guilt. It means release from the original guilt we experienced at the time of the separation and have continually re-experienced ever since. We should not feel guilty about that because we haven't really separated from God. We just think that we have because we are trapped in this illusory world. We should also not use guilt as a weapon against others because in doing so we will be hurting ourselves just as much. It is easy, when one is upset, to try to make the person involved feel guilty, but this tactic is simply an ego device that will continue to trap us. We have to watch our words very carefully to make sure that they do not induce feelings of guilt in others. Also we have to refuse to entertain feelings of guilt ourselves, which can be rather difficult.

Yet another way of releasing ourselves from the ego's clutches is to think only loving thoughts about others, and this, too, takes a lot of practice. But the *Course* tells us that if others attack us, it really is a cry for help because everything is based on either love or fear. *"Fear and love are the only emotions of which you are capable."* [219] Therefore anything unloving is based on fear. We can see this in ourselves when we attack others and we can see it in others when they attack us. But what we have to do in both cases is to react in a loving way and seek the help

---

[217] *ACIM,* T349.
[218] *ACIM,* T261.
[219] *ACIM,* T217.

of the Holy Spirit in this. *"Fear is a symptom of your own deep sense of loss. If when you perceive it in others you learn to supply the loss* (i.e., react in a loving manner), *the basic cause of fear is removed. Thereby you teach yourself that fear does not exist in you. The means for removing it is in yourself, and you have demonstrated this by giving it."* [220]

Forgiveness comes into the process of overcoming the ego because it is through forgiveness that we overlook anything that happened in the past and also because forgiving is a loving reaction that helps eradicate fear. Furthermore, if we are forgiving, it means we have embraced the Holy Spirit's "holy instant," which is the foremost weapon to use against the ego.

There is yet another weapon we can use to stamp out the ego: reason. *"The introduction of reason into the ego's thought system is the beginning of its undoing, for reason and the ego are contradictory. Nor is it possible for them to coexist in your awareness. For reason's goal is to make plain, and therefore obvious....The ego's whole continuance depends on its belief you cannot learn this Course. Share this belief, and reason will be unable to see your errors and make way for their correction. For reason sees through errors, telling you what you thought was real is not."* [221] Well that is certainly one good reason for us to make sure we do learn the *Course*. And this requires using our logical mind to study all the lessons and explanations and coming to the realisation that it all makes sense. If what is being taught also appeals to our intuitive minds, then all the better.

So how does reason help us in our battle? It awakens us from the dream by alerting us to the fact that life in this world is all an illusion and cannot possibly be the truth. *"How does one overcome illusions? Surely not by force or anger, nor by opposing them in any way. Merely by letting reason tell you that they contradict reality. They go against what must be true."* [222] One of the lessons in the Workbook deals with this subject. *"The ego makes illusions. Truth undoes its evil dreams by shining them away."* [223] So the search for truth is an important weapon against the ego.

---

[220] *ACIM,* T217.
[221] *ACIM,* T474 & 475.
[222] *ACIM,* T478.
[223] *ACIM,* W468, Lesson 332.

But with reason we can only go so far along the road to enlightenment. It won't take us the whole way. *"Reason is not salvation in itself, but it makes way for peace and brings you to a state of mind in which salvation can be given you. Sin (error of perception) is a block, set like a heavy gate, locked and without a key, across the road to peace. No one who looks on it without the help of reason would try to pass it.... Yet reason sees through it easily, because it is an error."* [224] Then we are told that the eyes of the physical body can only see physical things or form and they therefore keep us trapped in the world of form. On page 475 of the Text we read, *"These eyes, made not to see, will never see."* I think this means we will never have *spiritual* vision with our physical eyes. However, by using our logical mind or reason, through the study of the *Course*, we will realise that the world of matter or form is not real. *"Reason will tell you that if form is not reality it must be an illusion, and is not there to see. And if you see it you must be mistaken, for you are seeing what can **not** be real as if it were."* [225] So it is now up to us to decide whether we want to keep on deluding ourselves or whether we want to correct our perceptions of this world. If we choose the latter, the Holy Spirit is there to guide us.

If we choose instead to believe in the physical world—the world of the ego—we will ultimately suffer. Feelings of depression, deprivation or anger may follow. *"To identify with the ego is to attack yourself and make yourself poor. That is why everyone who identifies with the ego feels deprived. What he experiences then is depression or anger, because what he did was to exchange Self-love for self-hate, making him afraid of himself. He does not realize this."* [226]

I have a friend who is a very genuine and spiritual person, yet she always seems to be very unhappy. Whenever I talk to her on the phone she is always on the verge of travelling somewhere or escaping to another country. She seems to be running away but is not, at the conscious level, aware of this. She sounds irritated and sad and her latest wish is to go to some distant island where, *"things will be better."* I believe that, at some level, she realises that this world is an illusion and she is trying to escape from it. I would like to introduce her to the *Course* one day, but at the present time she is so uptight and unhappy that I don't

---

[224] *ACIM*, T475.

[225] *ACIM*, T476

[226] *ACIM*, T221.

think it would help her.

Hindus and Buddhists emphasise the need for a spiritual teacher or enlightened person to guide the disciple and help him overcome the ego. Similarly, *ACIM* teaches that we need the help of a teacher. *"There are areas in your learning skills that are so impaired that you can progress only under constant, clear-cut direction, provided by a Teacher, Who can transcend your limited resources. He becomes your Resource because of yourself you cannot learn."* [227] And if we follow this Teacher, who is the Holy Spirit, He will lead us back to God. *"The Holy Spirit is your strength because He knows nothing but the spirit as you. He is perfectly aware that you do not know yourself, and perfectly aware of how to teach you to remember what you are...To open the eyes of the blind is the Holy Spirit's mission, for He knows that they have not lost their vision, but merely sleep....The Holy Spirit keeps the vision of Christ for every Son of God who sleeps."* [228] One way of calling upon this great Teacher is to repeat Lessons 361 to 365 frequently. I repeat the following teaching every night before going to sleep. But, more importantly, I use it during the day whenever I feel at conflict about something or other. I have mentioned this lesson before but I would like to repeat it here because it is so important:

> *This holy instant would I give to You.*
>
> *Be You in charge. For I would follow You,*
>
> *Certain that Your direction gives me peace.*

There are a number of *ACIM* lessons that are very helpful when it comes to undoing the ego. One of them is Lesson 128: *"The world I see holds nothing that I want"* and the other is Lesson 129, *"Beyond this world there is a world I want."* Lesson 129 helps us look beyond this world, even though there are many things in it that appear to be attractive and pleasurable. What we have to realise is that all that is pleasurable will not remain that way, although there is no harm in enjoying it whilst it is available. *"The world you see is merciless indeed, unstable, cruel, unconcerned with you, quick to avenge and pitiless with hate. It gives but to*

---

[227] *ACIM*, T226.
[228] *ACIM*, T227 & 228.

rescind, and takes away all things that you have cherished for a while. No lasting love is found, for none is here. This is the world of time, where all things end." [229]

Think about it. All things you once loved have either been taken from you or definitely will be at some future point in time. How could this be the creation of a loving God? I feel this so acutely at the present moment because I put my beloved cat to sleep only two days ago. He had suffered from a debilitating disease for seven weeks, which forced him to cut back drastically on food and culminated in him refusing to eat a single morsel for nearly six days. I watched in great grief as his once vibrant, strong, healthy body, literally withered away before my eyes. All I could tell myself was, *"God did not create a meaningless world."* It felt as though I had been stabbed through the heart with a knife. Peace only returned to me when I watched him go to sleep and leave behind his pain-racked body. But the grief lives on in my heart. How clearly do I now understand the passage above that emphasises that this world, *"gives but to rescind, and takes away all things that you have cherished for a while...."* How could I believe in the world of the ego that really does appear to be cruel and pitiless? I did keep telling myself that it was all an illusion and that both the cat and I were not really living here in our physical bodies in this world and that it was really only a dream or a nightmare. But that did not take away the pain and it did not bring the nightmare to an end. I also told myself that what was suffering was my lower self or the wrong part of the mind because that is the only part of the mind that can experience loss. My higher self or spirit was possibly united right now with the spirit of my departed cat, but it was only his physical form that was no longer here. However, I do feel that while we are living here in the world of the ego, it is important to go through the grieving process and then beyond it. We can't deny grief even if it does come from the world of the ego. It feels so real.

A young boy in the school where I work asked me recently why animals have such short lives. He had a dog and cat that he loved but was aware that they would not be around for very long. I shook my head and said I did not know why. I couldn't think of a reply. I couldn't think of a single, sensible reason as to why our pets have such short life spans.

---

[229] *ACIM,* W235.

Lesson 129, entitled *"Beyond this world there is a world I want,"* points the way to God. *"Here is the world that comes to take its place, as you unbind your mind from little things the world sets forth to keep you prisoner. Value them not, and they will disappear. Esteem them, and they will seem real to you...Today the lights of Heaven bend to you, to shine upon your eyelids as you rest beyond the world of darkness. Here is light your eyes can not behold. And yet your mind can see it plainly, and can understand....This day we realize that what you feared to lose was only loss."* This last sentence is vital. All that we have been given in this world will end up as some form of loss. We either lose those we love when they die, or we die and so those who love us experience loss. We may experience a happy marriage, a joyful family, a rewarding career or lucrative business. But in the end we lose them all in one way or another. Such is the world of the ego. But what this passage is also saying is that, if we are worried about giving things up when we overcome the ego, the only thing we will really give up is loss.

The *Course* explains why we inevitably experience death and loss in the ego's world. *"The death penalty is the ego's ultimate goal, for it fully believes that you are a criminal, as deserving of death as God knows you are deserving of life. The death penalty never leaves the ego's mind, for that is what it always reserves for you in the end. Wanting to kill you as the final expression of its feeling for you, it lets you live but to await death. It will torment you while you live, but its hatred is not satisfied until you die. For your destructions is the one end toward which it works, and the only end with which it will be satisfied."* [230] This is because the ego believes that it has been treacherous to God because of the separation, and therefore deserves death. And that is why it is very important not to feel guilty because feelings of guilt stem only from the ego. Our task is to ignore the voice of the ego and listen only to that of the Holy Spirit.

What we must remember whenever we suffer is that it is all a dream and it is not really happening. This is not at all easy as I well know. *"The secret of salvation is but this; that you are doing this unto yourself....Whatever seems to be the cause of any pain and suffering you feel, this is still true. For you would not react at all to figures in a dream you know that you were dreaming....This single lesson learned will set you free*

---

[230] *ACIM*, T232 & 233.

from suffering, whatever form it takes...Bring, then, all forms of suffering to Him Who knows that every one is like the rest....When you forgive the world your guilt, you will be free of it..." [231] We have to somehow remember, whenever we experience any suffering or loss, that we have caused this pain to ourselves because of the guilt that is embedded deep in our subconscious minds. We also have to remember that it is as real as a dream and that the way to awaken from the nightmare is to listen to the Voice of the Holy Spirit. And even if we do not hear Him speak directly to us, His guidance will come in one way or another. It could be a flash of inspiration or a feeling of strength that comes as you experience a difficult moment or a dream or the words of a friend or guidance in a book. He will speak to us if we call upon Him. *"God's Voice speaks to me all through the day."* [232]

Let me return again to the subject of my cat. I called upon the Holy Spirit frequently (as well as the angels and archangels) in those last difficult days of his life. I did not know how I was going to get the strength to take him to the vet on my own and put him to sleep. Somehow I managed to. I think the Holy Spirit did give me the strength I needed. The reader may think I have made a mountain out of a molehill, but animal lovers will appreciate how upsetting it is to take one's pet to the vet for the last time so as to put it to sleep. It is so difficult to say goodbye to a beloved animal companion—a creature that is capable of so much unconditional love and devotion. It is even more difficult if you live alone with that pet and there's just you and it in your home. A strong bond just has to develop, if you love animals, and so naturally feelings of loss will be experienced. But time heals on this plane, thankfully. How lovely will it be to go where there is no time, no space and all of us are united as one. Finally we will be able to say goodbye to the duality of this illusory world—to the yin and the yang and the endless rounds of pleasure and pain.

I wanted to understand my loss and grief from the perspective of *ACIM*. So I logged on to a most useful website set up by the *Foundation for A Course in Miracles* and went onto its outreach section that answers questions sent in by *Course* students. It is an absolute mine of information and a wonderful resource:

---

[231] *ACIM*, T588.
[232] *ACIM*, W78.

www.facimoutreach.org I looked up the section on pets and animals and I *did* find something that brought me great comfort. A number of people had written in asking about how they could come to terms with the illness and loss of a pet. In the answers to the questions it was explained that due to the separation, we project guilt, fear and anger from our minds to the body, i.e., to our bodies or the bodies of other adults, children or animals. This may result in sickness and would explain why children and animals get sick. But we can ask the Holy Spirit to heal our minds and correct our perceptions and this could lead to the recovery of those who are ill. As for the death of a cat which one student had found difficult to come to terms with, just as I had, it was explained that the cat's body, like our body, neither lives nor dies, and that minds are joined without the body's interference. Therefore the cat is no more or less real now than when it appeared to be physically present, and because all minds are joined, the connection with the mind of the pet could be maintained after death. If there is a strong bond of love between a cat and its owner, nothing, including death, can deprive that person of that love. It was also suggested that the cat could be viewed as a symbol of guilt, from the ego's point of view, but from the Holy Spirit's point of view that cat could become a symbol of love and forgiveness. A lot more was written about the relationship between people and their pets and I would recommend anyone interested to visit that website.

Then I searched through *ACIM* to try to find a way of reinterpreting death. I found a very interesting discussion about death in the Manual. It was explained that all illusions stem from death because it is the symbol of the fear of God. How could a loving God cause us to be born, grow old, become ill and then die? He couldn't. We accept this process as being *"the way of nature"* but only a cruel creator could do this to us. But for the ego, which does not believe in a loving God and, in fact, lives in fear of God, death seems very real. Furthermore, death can only affect bodies, so if we believe we are a body, then we believe that we will die. The following passage really did help me come to terms with the death of my pet. *"God is, and in Him all created things must be eternal...Accept no compromise in which death plays a part. Do not believe in cruelty, nor let attack conceal the truth from you. What seems to die has but been misperceived and carried to illusion. Now it becomes your task to let the illusion be carried to the truth. Be steadfast but in this; be not deceived by the "reality" of any changing form. Truth neither moves nor wavers nor sinks down to death and dissolution. And what is the end of death? Nothing but this; the realization that the Son of God is guiltless now and forever. Nothing but this."* [233] So, as I buried my cat's ashes in the garden, I told myself that although he seemed to have died, he hadn't. His form had appeared to change but his body was not real just as mine is not. However, I like to think of my cat as part of the one joined mind, which we all share. In this way I feel that he hasn't really departed at all and that our bond of love will keep us connected in some way.

Well, to return to the topic of overcoming the ego, one day I decided to write down every feeling or thought that stemmed from the ego and log it in a notebook that I carried around with me. Well, it was really rather depressing, because as soon as I woke up there were thoughts in my mind that weren't too positive, and so I had to enter them into the logbook. When I got to work there were plenty more occasions when the ego reared its head and by the end of the day I had quite a few entries in that logbook. Needless to say, I discarded it after that! But I do constantly watch my thoughts and feelings and I am well aware that all the unpleasant ones stem from the ego.

When you understand the extent of the grip that the ego has on human beings it becomes much easier to understand human behaviour. You realise that, for instance, when one person lashes out at another or puts down another, this is merely his ego projecting its fears, guilt and inadequacies onto others so that he can feel better about himself. A person who seems to be very controlling is simple being ruled by an ego that is fighting for power to ensure its own survival. This is because the ego has created a finite and limited world and it therefore believes there is not enough of everything to go around. So it tries to grab as much as possible for itself. This could be money, power, possessions, the attention of another etc. Actually, all the rivalry that we see in the world stems from the ego, i.e., sibling rivalry, jealousy between school children, competitiveness between sportsmen and rivalry at the work place and at the national and international levels. So *ACIM* can be seen as being a course on both spirituality and psychology because it gives us a very good insight into the whys

---

[233] *ACIM*, M67.

and wherefores of all human behaviour. And if we remember that we are motivated either by love or by fear, then we realise that the majority of human actions and reactions are based on fear. A quick glance at a newspaper would be enough to prove that they are usually not based on love.

Now I would like to take a look at how a number of authors and teachers have dealt with the subject of undoing the ego. The Tibetan meditation master and teacher Chogyam Trungpa in his book, which I mentioned earlier, *Cutting Through Spiritual Materialism*, says that we have to look at our neurotic thoughts and emotions and realise they are false concepts that stem from the ego. Then we remove these concepts by realising that all around is nothing but emptiness or *sunyata*. I think he means that we have to just turn away from unhappy thoughts because they are not real. This is a difficult thing to do but if we try persistently we will get better at doing it.

In his commentary on *The Heart Sutra*, Edward Conze refers to the unreliability of the ego, which he says can only find security by looking for external supports to sustain it. *"This tendency is rooted in the very fibers of our being. The kind of mental life which springs from ignorance seeks forever to build a fictitious security on what is in fact quite unstable and untrustworthy."* [234]

Sogyal Rinpoche, in his book *The Tibetan Book of Living and Dying*, describes the ego as, *"garrulous, demanding, hysterical and calculating,"* and he contrasts it with the *"still voice of wisdom"* that is within us. He explains that by listening to this voice of wisdom one is able to overcome the ego. *"Gradually you will find yourself able to free yourself more and more quickly from the dark emotions that have ruled your life, and this ability to do so is the greatest miracle of all."* [235]

We are all very busy these days, and I am no exception. But why is it that we are determined to fill up every hour and every minute of our lives? Is it because we are afraid of being alone with our thoughts? I know that sometimes I switch on the radio simply to shut out the mental chatter that is going on in my mind.

---

[234] Edward Conze, *Buddhist Wisdom – The Diamond Sutra and the Heart Sutra* pp. 103-104, Vintage Books, Random House Inc., 2001.

[235] Sogyal Rinpoche, *The Tibetan Book of Living and Dying*, p. 120, © 1992, published by Rider. Reprinted by permission of The Random House Group Ltd & HarperCollins Publishers.

On the rare occasion when I have absolutely nothing to do, I find myself doing something around the house such as washing the bedspread or curtains! And then if I have nothing to do at all I either read or watch TV. It is rare for me to just sit down and "be," but I am working on it and I think my regular meditation time in the morning is useful because when you meditate you cannot do anything else.

The philosopher and author Wei Wu Wei warned that being excessively busy was a ploy of the ego. *"Doing—work and distraction (distraction from what?)— constitute a screen between the apparent 'I' and the real 'I.'"* By "apparent I" he is referring to the non-existent ego and the "real I" is what he calls the "universal Mind." Wei Wu Wei explains that the ego has to be continually busy in order to protect its existence. *"...it is from fear of the destruction of this illusory personality that he dare not face up to his real self in silence and the awareness of Being."*[236]

I have now come to realise that idleness is not such a bad thing. The problem is people sometimes feel guilty when just sitting down doing nothing. I am not sure why that is. Maybe it has something to with the Protestant work ethic that has remained in our subconscious minds since the 16th century. In any case, I now consciously sit down and remain idle for short periods of time and don't feel at all guilty. It's a lovely thing to do on a Sunday morning whilst lying in bed and gazing out at the trees.

The ego is our enemy that has to be vanquished said the Indian sage Shankara. *"...Turn inwards all the thought-forms that adhere to the ego. He is an enemy of yours, so kill him with the sword of knowledge. He has been harming you like a thorn in your throat while eating. Give up all desires in order to realize your state as the supreme Self....The ego may in this way be killed, but if thought is given to it even for a moment it revives and engages in activity, driving a man before it as the wind drives winter clouds...the ego revives through thoughts of sense objects."* [237] And we are advised to look upon everything in the universe as Brahmin or God so that the

---

[236] Wei Wu Wei, *Fingers Pointing towards the Moon*, pp. 36-37, First Sentient Publications, Colorado, USA, 2003.

[237] Ramana Maharshi and Shankara, *Ramana, Shankara and the Forty Verses, The Essential Teachings of Advaita*, pp. 45-46, *Watkins* Publishing, London 2002.

ego will eventually disappear.

Ramana Maharshi advised his followers to reflect upon the ephemeral nature of external phenomenon as this would make it easier to turn away from the external world. He called this enquiry into the nature of things, *vichara*, and said, *"When vichara continues automatically and continuously, it will see the impermanence and, therefore the futility of and aversion to wealth, fame, ease, pleasure, etc."* [238]

K. R. Paramahamsa suggests that one should live in the present in order to overcome the ego. This is good advice, as we saw in Chapter 6. *"When the mind stops linking to the past and the future, it becomes no-mind. If from moment to moment, one's mind dwells on what is, and drops it effortlessly at once, the mind becomes no-mind, full of purity."* [239] He also said that complete freedom from desire, hope or expectation in regard to objects was another good way to subdue the mind and hence the ego.

Now I would like to talk about vertigo. Why? Because it may be a very good sign. When I was almost two thirds of the way through *ACIM* Workbook lessons I decided to read Gary Renard's excellent book, *The Disappearance of the Universe*, which I mentioned earlier. Whilst I was reading that book I suddenly developed an inexplicable giddiness which lasted for ten days. I remember sitting on the sofa, clutching my stomach as the walls of the room seemed to slowly rotate. Yet, funnily enough, I didn't feel ill enough to go to the doctor, although I had suffered from vertigo quite seriously several years before and had to have medication for it then. But this time it felt different. There was just this spinning in my head that lasted on and off for several days. Then, luckily for me, it vanished as suddenly as it had started. It wasn't until I read Gary Renard's second book that I understood what the vertigo had been all about. In *Your Immortal Reality* on page 108, he explains that he had heard from readers who had experienced vertigo whilst they were reading *The Disappearance of the Universe*. He also said that he himself had suffered from vertigo when he was doing the exercises in the Workbook. Suddenly it all made sense to me. I had

---

[238] Nagesh D. Sonde, *Philosophy of Bhagavan Sri Ramana Maharishi*, p. 55, Sri Satguru Publications, Delhi, 2005.

[239] K. R. Paramahamsa, *Tat Sat*, p. 19, Total Recall Publications, Inc. Texas.

suffered from vertigo when I understood exactly what *ACIM* was saying, because it was such a radical change of perception and it threw my ego off course. Maybe it came as a shock to my ego to suddenly see me question its existence. The reason it happened when I read Gary Renard's book was that it gave the most excellent interpretation of the *Course* so that suddenly all that I had been studying for the previous nine months had been clarified in my mind. Many of the questions that I had regarding *ACIM* had now been answered and I was ready to take it all on board and (hopefully) apply it in my own life. My ego reacted violently and, as was to be expected, gave me a hard time. These teachings were so different from what I had been brought up to believe that it was not surprising that I experienced the vertigo that I did. This was the *"sense of actual disorientation"* that the *Course* warned about. So, why was that a good thing? Because it showed me that I was not stuck in a rut, believing that all the illusions around me were real. I was ready to wake up and accept the truth, however different it was from my former beliefs.

I have another tactic for avoiding the traps set up by the ego. I am very careful about what sort of music I listen to. Although I do love some popular and rock music, especially Bruce Springsteen's songs, these days I try to listen to classical music more than other types of music. The trouble with pop songs is that they keep you stuck in time because they remind you of a place or a person who you were with when you heard a particular song previously. So they can keep you stuck in the past. Or the lyrics deal with some awful tragedy such as your loved one walking away from you and therefore you experience feelings of sadness and loss, which of course could only be coming from the ego. Alternatively, they may make you feel lonely and unloved because you are not in a relationship, whereas the lyrics are about a happy pair of lovers. And of course again this is just another way of the ego trying to surface and make you feel incomplete on your own. We are completely whole on our own and unattached, and I think the only truly good relationship is one in which both partners feel whole and complete on their own, but are choosing to spend time together, not to complement each other, but because that is their preference.

As I have mentioned before I have had many relationships. Why did I feel the need to attach myself to a man? I don't really know. Perhaps the desire for union with a man is simply a reflection of the desire for a much greater union, the union between man and God? Or should I say reunion? Now, after having decided that relationships are a thing of the past for me, I realise that the union between a man and a woman is merely a pale imitation of the ultimate union between man and God. The desire for a man is the desire for an *"idol"* and a *"special relationship,"* to use the terminology of the *Course.* But no permanent union can ever be achieved between a man and a woman on the physical plane. Eventually one of them will either leave the relationship or die. Then the other one will follow suit. Yet, in the world of spirit, when we have returned Home, I believe there will be a much greater union of all beings with each other and with God. And it is useful to remember that although we appear to be men and women, this is just part of the illusion. In the world of spirit there is no gender; gender is yet another of the ego's fabrications. This is what I remind myself if ever I feel tempted to embark on another relationship. *"Remember,"* I tell myself, *"it's all an illusion."* Yes, all of it. The romantic meals out, the wonderful, fun-filled holidays, and the moments of passion will all come to an end—and *they are not the goal of life* despite what the media would like us to believe. Switch on the radio or television on Valentine's Day and you will feel quite inadequate for being the only person on the planet who is not in a relationship, or so it seems.

ACIM calls anything that we desire in the physical world an *"idol"* and explains, *"Behind the search for every idol lies the yearning for completion. Wholeness has no form because it is unlimited. To seek a special person or a thing to add to you to make yourself complete, can only mean that you believe some form is missing. And by finding this, you will achieve completion in a form you like."* [240] And earlier on in the Text it is pointed out, *"The search for the special relationship is the sign that you equate yourself with the ego and not with God. For the special relationship has value only to the ego....When two individuals seek to become one, they are trying to decrease their magnitude. Each would deny his power, for the separate union excludes the universe. Far more is left outside than would be taken in, for God is left without and nothing taken in."* [241]

I know some happy couples can spend a lifetime in harmony together but if

---

[240] *ACIM*, T631.
[241] *ACIM*, T345.

that distracts them from the only real goal (i.e., enlightenment or awakening) then, in my opinion, it is a waste of a lifetime. *"...Every special relationship you have made has, as its fundamental purpose, the aim of occupying your mind so completely that you will not hear the call of truth."* [242]

Some couples journey back home to God together and that must be a wonderful experience. They have a *"holy relationship"*, in the terminology of the *Course*. But I don't think this type of relationship is all that common. A holy relationship is one in which two people join together with a common goal that takes them beyond the needs of their separate egos. They invite the Holy Spirit into the relationship and they have truth as their goal. Holy relationships are dealt with at length in the *Course*. *"The holy relationship is the expression of the holy instant in living in this world....The holy relationship, a major step toward the perception of the real world, is learned. It is the old, unholy relationship, transformed and seen anew."*[243] Those in a holy relationship have offered their relationship to the Holy Spirit to use for His purposes. They have joined together at the level of the mind and not the body and the holiness within the relationship benefits others, as well as themselves. *"When you accepted truth as the goal for your relationship, you became a giver of peace as surely as your Father gave peace to you...."*[244]

I should add that I believe love between a man and a woman does have a place in our society, *within the illusion*, but only during a certain stage in our lives. Romantic love, which binds a couple together and is followed by a family, is a wonderful thing. The best thing we can give children is a happy, harmonious and loving two-parent family, if possible. But later on in life, when the children have grown up, I don't think it is "the end of the world" if the relationship comes to an end when one (or both) partners decide to move onto a different lifestyle. Maybe they now realise that they should dedicate their lives to the return to God. If they can do that together, in a holy relationship, then that is wonderful. If they choose to do it apart, well I think it is equally wonderful. In Hinduism, according to the Code of Manu, it is believed that the spiritual-seeker goes through four stages of life. In the first stage he is a student; in the second stage he is a

---

[242] *ACIM*, T358.
[243] *ACIM*, T362.
[244] *ACIM*, T371.

householder and it is in this stage of life that he marries and raises children. He may become a "forest-dweller" in the third stage, and this is when he leaves his family and goes away to worship God and meditate. Finally, in the fourth stage he renounces all his former ties and becomes free from worldly desires and attachments. Now he is free to wander around wherever he wishes, having achieved liberation.

"The permanent association of one man and one woman, though it may conceivably have some social utility, appears to be a hindrance to the adequate utilisation of a life, and so to full temporal realisation." [245] said that wonderful sage Wei Wu Wei.

In the Dhammapada we read, *"So long as the love of man towards women, even the smallest, is not destroyed, so long is his mind in bondage, as the calf that drinks milk is to its mother."* [246]

I would like to end this chapter with the *Course's* comparison between the ego and the miracle because it shows that, for those who are weary of living in this illusory world, the miracle is really the only choice to make. *"What is the ego? Nothingness, but in a form that seems like something. In a world of form the ego cannot be denied for it alone seems real. Yet could God's son as He created him abide in form or in a world of form? Who asks you to define the ego and explain how it arose can be but he who thinks it real..."* [247] This last sentence explains why it is pointless to ask about the nature of the ego because it is not real and therefore has no nature. Only those who believe in the ego would ask such a question. As for a miracle, it is, *"The ego's opposite in every way, in origin, effect and consequence....Where there was darkness now we see the light. What is the ego? What the darkness was. Where is the ego? Where the darkness was. What is it now and where can it be found? Nothing and nowhere. Now the light has come: Its opposite has gone without a trace. Where evil was there now is holiness."* [248] And that is what disciples are striving for—to see the ego vanish without a trace so that the light of God can shine through.

---

[245] Wei Wu Wei, *Fingers Pointing towards the Moon*, p. 65, First Sentient Publications, Colorado, USA, 2003.

[246] *Dhammapada – A Collection of Verses from the Pali Canon of Buddhism*, p. 64, Chapter 20, verse 284, translated by F Max Muller, Red & Black Publishers, Florida, 2008.

[247] *ACIM*, M81.

[248] *ACIM*, M81.

Chapter 8

It's All An Illusion—So What?

"Man has come here with a definite purpose. Life is not meant for eating, drinking, dressing and procreating." [249]

I imagine some readers by now may feel like asking, *"OK, we understand that it's all an illusion, but why don't we just get on and enjoy our lives anyway?"* That is a very valid question and the answer depends on what you think the purpose of your life is. I have spent a large portion of my life just living it and enjoying it, but for many years I have felt that I have a loftier life purpose. We all have. So whilst there's nothing wrong with living life and enjoying it, one may find that one's goals in life change over time. Personally speaking, my own goals have changed quite dramatically in the past few years. Now all that really matters to me is salvation, enlightenment, or liberation from the cycle of birth, death and rebirth, whatever you want to call it. In order to achieve that, I have to awaken from the dream. I have to really know that *it's all an illusion* so that I can do something about it; otherwise I will be trapped here forever and that is one thing I am determined not to be. Imagine reaching the end of your lifetime, looking back at all you did and realising that you had wasted it on trivialities and that actually you are no further forward than you were when you were born. What a horrible thought!

---

[249] Swami Sivananda, *Bliss Divine – A Book of Spiritual Essays on the Lofty Purpose of Human Life and the Means to its Achievement*, p. 511, compiled by Sri Ananthanarayanan, The Divine Life Society, Himalayas, India, 2006.

"*Freedom from illusions lies only in not believing them,*" [250] we are taught in *ACIM*. So in order to not believe in them, we have first to be aware of them. Hence the importance of studying this topic and this is one of the reasons for the writing of this book. We need to *know* about the illusions if we are to succeed in overcoming them. "*No one can escape from illusions unless he looks at them, for not looking is the way they are protected.*" [251]

Elsewhere in the *Course* we read, "*All that you need to give this world away in glad exchange for what you did not make, is willingness to learn the one you made is false.*" [252] So one of the most important things we can do for ourselves is to have an open mind and be ready to change all our beliefs, so that we are open to the truth and therefore ready to move beyond the illusions that are keeping us ensnared. The following uplifting passage shows that doing so will indeed be worthwhile: "*Those who let illusions be lifted from their minds are this world's saviors, walking the world with their Redeemer, and carrying His message of hope and freedom and release from suffering to everyone who needs a miracle to save him.*" [253] Offering hope and freedom to others is surely a worthy way to live one's life.

Time and again in *ACIM* we are advised to correct our perceptions from illusions to truth. "*Illusions are but beliefs in what is not there. And the seeming conflict between truth and illusion can only be resolved by separating yourself from the illusion and not from truth.*" [254]

A number of *Course* lessons deal with the need to recognize the illusion. Lesson 226 tells us that we should hasten home and that the only way to do so is to become aware of the illusions. Death is no escape. Changing our perceptions of the world is the only way to freedom. "*If I believe it* (the world) *has a value as I see it now, so will it still remain for me. But if I see no value in the world as I behold it, nothing that I want to keep as mine or search for as a goal, it will depart from me. For I have not sought for illusions to replace the truth.*" And the prayer that follows asks, "*What need have I to linger in a place of vain desires and of shattered dreams, when*

---

[250] *ACIM* T154.

[251] *ACIM,* T202.

[252] *ACIM,* T254.

[253] *ACIM,* T478.

[254] *ACIM,* T336.

Heaven can so easily be mine?" [255] So easily? Wow!

The following lesson also deals with the renunciation of illusions. *"...I am free because I was mistaken, and did not affect my own reality at all by my illusions. Now I give them up, and lay them down before the feet of truth, to be removed forever from my mind. This is my holy instant of release..."* [256]

The *Course* frequently emphasises throughout its many pages that the ego and the body are all part of the illusion and need to be relinquished. On page 131 of the Text we read, *"The whole purpose of this Course is to teach you that the ego is unbelievable and will forever be unbelievable...."* and on page 299 of the Workbook we are told that we can attain the vision of Christ but it means realising that our bodies are not real. *"Christ's vision has one law. It does not look upon a body, and mistake it for the Son whom God created. It beholds a light beyond the body; an idea beyond what can be touched, a purity undimmed by errors, pitiful mistakes, and fearful thoughts of guilt from dreams of sin. It sees no separation. And it looks on everyone, on every circumstance, all happenings and all events, without the slightest fading of the light it sees."* I have started to look at people and try to see the light within them instead of focusing on the words their egos speak and the deeds their egos perform. This is what Jesus would like us to do because he stresses, *"See no one as a body. Greet him as the Son of God he is, acknowledging that he is one with you in holiness."* [257]

We need to see the light within others or to see them as spirit rather than bodies because this gives both them and us freedom. *"You are not limited by the body, and thought cannot be made flesh. Yet mind can be manifested through the body if it goes beyond it and does not interpret it as limitation. Whenever you see another as limited to or by the body, you are imposing this limit on yourself. Are you willing to accept this, when your whole purpose for learning should be to escape from limitations?"* [258] If this seems difficult to do, remember that we have the Holy Spirit here to help us. *"Created by God, He left neither God nor His creation. He is both God and you,*

---

[255] *ACIM*, W404, Lesson 226.
[256] *ACIM*, W405, Lesson 227.
[257] *ACIM*, W299, Lesson 158.
[258] *ACIM*, T154.

as you are God and Him together. For God's Answer to the separation added more to you than tried to take away...." [259] As the Holy Spirit remains with us and is our direct link to God, Who better to ask for guidance and for strength?

So, we can see how important it is to recognize that our world is an illusory one and to then search for a way of finding the truth. But *ACIM* is not the only Path to God and there could be instances when knowing about the illusion may *not* be important. If, for example, one practises love and forgiveness all the time, like Mahatma Gandhi (1869–1948) or Mother Teresa (1910– 1997) then, knowledge about the illusory world is redundant. They practised the teachings of *ACIM* without even knowing about them. Perhaps they *were* able to break the cycle of birth and death and attain liberation through their adherence to non-violence, simplicity and truth, and, in the case of Mother Teresa, to her altruistic deeds. But how many of us do that? How many of us are like Mother Teresa? How many of us live lives of total selflessness, of love and of complete forgiveness without having any material needs? Probably no more than a tiny minority of us live like that. So for the vast majority of us, *knowledge about the illusions* and how to overcome them, i.e., through practising love and forgiveness, *is* helpful. I believe, in fact, that it is vital. One could say that the first step in the *Course* is to recognize the illusion and the second step is to take practical measures to overcome it. This consists of learning the lessons and above all of practicing forgiveness and being non-judgemental.

Some teachers have spoken about the need to use the mind as a tool to help us overcome ignorance and find the truth. The Indian yogi Sri Ramana Maharishi encouraged his disciples to practice self-enquiry and he explained that one cannot *attain* the Self or Atman because it is always as it is. However, *"....all that is necessary is to be aware of the veil which obscures the 'I', the Self from Brahman, and give up considering the Ego which is the non-self, as the Self, the unreal as the Real. When we give up such erroneous identification of our Self with the body, the Self alone remains."* [260] So we can see that the Indian sage stressed quite clearly that it is wrong to identify with the ego as it is unreal. In other words we need to

---

[259] *ACIM,* T336.

[260] Nagesh D. Sonde, *Philosophy of Bhagavan Sri Ramana Maharishi,* p. 37, Sri Satguru Publications, Delhi, 2005.

distinguish between illusions and the truth. In his teachings he said enquiry about the nature of the Self was important so that one becomes aware of whom one is referring to when one uses the pronoun "I." He said the "I" is not the body but is something within the body. There is an "I" that comes and goes and that one is aware of as soon as one awakens in the morning. But he said there is another "I" that exists independently from the body, for instance, when one is asleep. "Which is the real one?" he asked his disciples. Then he explained to them, *"The crux of the enquiry is the realisation that the 'I' which comes and goes is the ego, influenced by the senses during each of the states* (i.e., waking, dreaming and deep sleep), *whereas the 'I' which ever is, is the Self. Then you will be aware that you are the Self. This is called Realisation.... The only error which the human being makes is that he forgets that he is the Self, which is unattached and ever blissful, and identifies himself with the ego, which is shaped by the sense contacts and influenced by the mind with all its thoughts, concepts, ideas, etc. To cease to identify oneself with the mind, is all that is required."* [261] Maharishi then said this was difficult for us to do because we have identified with the ego for such a long period of time.

The Zen teacher Bodhidharma also advocated enquiry into the nature of the Self. He said that, once one is aware of one's true nature, then one is a Buddha even if one works as a butcher! He was then asked how butchers, who slaughter animals and thereby create karma, could be buddhas. He replied, *"I only talk about seeing your nature. As long as a person creates karma, he keeps passing through birth and death. But once a person realizes his original nature, he stops creating karma. If he doesn't see his nature, invoking buddhas won't release him from his karma, regardless of whether or not he's a butcher. But once he sees his nature, all doubts vanish. Even a butcher's karma has no effect on such a person."* [262] His reference here to "seeing your nature" is, in my opinion, identical with determining the truth from illusion, the unreal from the real.

Indian author K.R. Paramahamsa also dwells on the importance of the investigation into the nature of the Self, in his book *Tat Sat*, although his beliefs differ somewhat from the teachings of *ACIM* as he places emphasis on

---

[261] Nagesh D. Sonde, *Philosophy of Bhagavan Sri Ramana Maharishi*, pp. 38-39, Sri Satguru Publications, Delhi, 2005.

[262] Red Pine, *The Zen Teaching of Bodhidharma*, p. 41, North Point Press, New York, 1989.

consciousness, which the *Course* does not. However, there are some similarities. He said the Lord/the Self is the intelligence that dwells in the human body. This Self is pure intelligence or Cosmic Intelligence in which there is no distinction between subject and object. *"He is the void in which the universe appears to exist. Only if one is firmly established in the unreality of the universe, like the blueness of the sky, can the Lord be realized. Dualism presupposes unity; non-dualism suggests dualism. Only when the creation is known to be utterly non-existent is the Lord realized."* [263] So here an analogy can be made with *ACIM*. But then Paramahamsa explains that the Self is consciousness and is not unreal, but rather it is the *"self of all"* that dwells within human beings and has no beginning and no end. Nevertheless, we see some similarity with the *Course* on page 71 of *Tat Sat*, *"The materiality of the creation is like the castle in the air, an illusory projection of one's mind – imaginary."*

I think it is important to bear in mind that although Hindu and Buddhist teachings differ in some aspects from the teachings of the *Course*, all three belief systems emphasize the need for introspection, contemplation and enquiry into the nature of the self. It is only in this way that one can come to a realisation of what is real and what is unreal and then, hopefully, overcome the unreal.

One lesson above all in the *Course* is particularly appealing to me. It is Lesson 199 in the Workbook: *"I am not a body. I am free."* This lesson explains that as long as we identify with our physical bodies we will never be free. The ego clings onto the belief that it *is* a body because this ensures its survival. *"Freedom must be impossible, as long as you perceive a body as yourself. The body is a limit...The mind can be made free when it no longer sees itself as in a body....The ego holds the body dear because it dwells in it, and lives united with the home that it has made. It is a part of the illusion that has sheltered it from being found illusory itself."* [264] It is precisely because the physical form, with its five senses, feels and appears to be so real that it is difficult to believe otherwise. Yet we have no option but to overcome this illusion if we are to be liberated and achieve enlightenment.

I have mentioned the wise Wei Wu Wei several times in this book. In the following passage he explains exactly why we need to become aware that we are

---

[263] K. R. Paramahamsa, *Tat Sat*, p. 34, Total Recall Publications, Inc. Texas, 2007.
[264] *ACIM*, W 382, Lesson 199.

living in an illusory world. *"One cannot get rid of one's apparent ego by throwing stones at it as if it were an importunate cur. It will only go when one comes to understand that it isn't there."* [265]

This of course makes perfect sense. The ego is deemed to be the enemy in our quest for enlightenment. How can we wage a war against it if we don't even realise that it is the enemy? That's why there is no way of avoiding study, logical thinking, self-enquiry and contemplation regardless of whether one is a follower of the teachings of Hinduism, Buddhism or *A Course in Miracles*.

The ego is the enemy firstly because it is unreal and secondly because it is at the root of all our troubles on this planet. As I have pointed out before, *ACIM* teaches us that there are really only two emotions: love and fear. Fear comes from the ego and love comes from God. Therefore, any activity that is not loving, such as verbal or physical abuse at the individual level, or acts of terrorism or war at the national and global levels, emanate from the ego. Looking at a TV news bulletin one day I realised that all the war-mongering heads of state and politicians, who send their young people out to kill in the name of national or economic security, and all the terrorist organisations of the world, which do pretty much the same thing, are all merely puppets of their egos. The ego feels insecure and so it tries to find security in every way possible. Being deluded, it believes that attacking and killing others is the way to preserve itself and its future. Nothing could be further from the truth. The laws of karma will make sure that anyone who goes out to kill anyone else will come to a sticky end himself. I should add, though, that killing in self-defence is an exception. One couldn't be expected to stand by, if physically attacked, and just let it happen.

Something else to bear in mind is that we attack and kill others because we judge them. The *Course* tells us that this sort of behaviour stems from our own guilt and it is *not* the will of God. *"Harm is the outcome of judgement. It is the dishonest act that follows a dishonest thought. It is a verdict of guilt upon a brother, and therefore on oneself. It is the end of peace and the denial of learning. It demonstrates the*

---

[265] Wei Wu Wei, *Fingers Pointing towards the Moon*, p. 32, First Sentient Publications, Colorado, USA, 2003.

absence of God's curriculum, and its replacement by insanity." [266] Whenever I observe on television the acts of violence that we perpetrate against each other, it seems to me that we have indeed gone insane.

Well to return to the topic of contemplation and understanding in the quest for liberation, *right understanding* comes at the top of the list of Buddha's *Eightfold Noble Path*. It refers to understanding the *Four Noble Truths*, which means understanding things as they really are. This entails becoming aware of illusions and discovering which path leads to the *end of suffering*, as Buddha put it. When a person has *right understanding* he realises that all things are transient and that desire for them leads to suffering. He also realises there is no self or ego. So *right understanding* is one of the tools to overcome ignorance.

Knowing that it's all an illusion is not an easy thing to do because we are living in a material world where all the emphasis seems to be on the acquisition of material goods and the comfort of the physical body. This is what we have been concerned about for aeons and so it is understandable that the teachings of the *Course* and of other sages fall on deaf ears.

Edward Conze in his commentary on the Diamond Sutra warns that disciples can be disheartened by the material world and, *"The enormous quantity of matter that we perceive around us, compared with the trembling little flicker of spiritual insight that we perceive within us, seems to tell strongly in favour of a materialistic outlook on life."* [267] But he points out, on the same page, that matter consists only of thoughts and words and, *"These material things have their roots in our own minds, and it is there that they can be uprooted."*

But we must not become dejected. We have but one choice to make and we must make it. The true disciple or spiritual seeker persists, knowing that his quest will ultimately bear fruit. And it should not be forgotten that we have a most powerful Guide to lean on when we feel lost who will lead us Home. The Holy Spirit—the Voice for God—is here with us, His only aim being to awaken us from our dreams and take us back to our Source. As Jesus says so eloquently,

---

[266] *ACIM*, M12 & 13.

[267] Edward Conze, *Buddhist Wisdom—The Diamond Sutra and the Heart Sutra*, p. 66, Vintage Books, Random House Inc, 2001.

towards the end of the Text, *"My brothers in salvation, do not fail to hear my voice and listen to my words. I ask for nothing but your own release....To your tired eyes I bring a vision of a different world, so new and clean and fresh you will forget the pain and sorrow that you saw before. Yet this is a vision which you must share with everyone you see, for otherwise you will behold it not. To give this gift is how to make it yours. And God ordained, in loving kindness that it be for you....In joyous welcome is my hand outstretched to every brother who would join with me in reaching past temptation,* (error) *and who looks with fixed determination toward the light that shines beyond in perfect constancy."* [268]

---

[268] *ACIM*, T668.

Chapter 9

Forgiveness

"Every act of forgiveness undoes the ego, and the Holy Spirit removes the blocks to the awareness of God, or spirit's presence." [269]

A Course in Miracles is, as I have mentioned before, the path of forgiveness or, as I call it, the yoga of forgiveness. Before taking an in-depth look at forgiveness and exploring *why* it is one of the ways one can return Home, I would like to draw a brief comparison between some of the teachings of *ACIM* and Christianity.

I am sure there are many readers who are sceptical about the teachings of *ACIM*, perhaps orthodox Christians more than any others. I know there are vast differences between these two major belief systems, but if we go beyond the differences I think some common ground can be found. So if I start with a look at the differences, I think a major one is the belief of God being a God of wrath and retribution who will be there to judge us at the end of time. This view is shared by a number of orthodox religions but *ACIM* stresses repeatedly that we have *not* sinned, even after the fall (or separation/splitting of the mind), and that we are indeed as holy as God is for the simple reason that God, being perfect, could only create perfection. The only thing we are really guilty of is ignorance and of being unaware that we are still at Home with God and Christ in Heaven. But a change of perception can rectify that problem with the help of the Holy Spirit or Jesus. I

---

[269] Gary Renard, *Your Immortal Reality*, p. 75, Hay House Inc., Carlsbad, CA, 2006.

feel that changing our perceptions by correcting the errors in our minds is the major goal of *ACIM*. However, another important objective of the *Course* is peace. This will ensue automatically if we are able to change our perceptions, awaken from the illusion and practice love and forgiveness. Peace follows in the footsteps of love and forgiveness. Strangely enough the *Course* teaches this the other way round. We are told that knowledge or the correction of errors in our minds actually follows in the footsteps of peace. *"Knowledge is not the motivation for learning this course. Peace is. This is the prerequisite for knowledge only because those who are in conflict are not peaceful, and peace is the condition of knowledge because it is the condition of the Kingdom. Knowledge can be restored only when you meet its conditions."* [270] My interpretation of this passage is that we are not at peace because we are living in the world of the ego, which is a world of chaos and conflict. When we become loving and peaceful by following the teachings of the *Course*, we are able to undo the errors in our minds and remember our true nature before the separation. That is why the word *"restored"* is used.

I think it is true to say that some followers of the orthodox religions, including Christianity, believe that only those who practise *their* religion will go to Heaven in the end. The rest of us are doomed to perish in hell. *ACIM* tells us there is no hell, except on earth, and that one day, when we have all "awoken" from our illusions, we will all dwell together in Heaven, all joined and one with each other and with God and Christ. *"Until you choose Heaven, you are in hell and misery."* [271] Clearly hell is something we made up when we made up the ego, the universe and everything in it. I think hell was invented by the ego probably because of its inherent feelings of guilt. But to me hell only exists in this world because living a life of illusion is like living in hell. It may not be boiling hot all the time but it's like being trapped in a place and in circumstances from which there appears to be no escape. Fortunately, there *is* a means of escape. *ACIM* tells us that the way out of hell is to listen to the Holy Spirit. *"Do not, then, think that following the Holy Spirit's guidance is necessary merely because of your own inadequacies. It is the way of out of hell for you."* [272]

---

[270] *ACIM*, T138.

[271] *ACIM*, T473.

[272] *ACIM*, M70.

I think another major difference is that the followers of Christianity believe that only Christians can call upon Jesus and the Holy Spirit. However, *ACIM* leads us to believe that *anyone* can do so, regardless of their religion or lack of it, and we are told that all are equal in the eyes of God. And however "special" we may feel we are, or feel our religion is, we are all going to be dwelling together in one melting pot when we ascend to Heaven (or awaken from the dream), regardless of the religion we have or have not followed whilst appearing to be here on earth. *"The Second Coming is the time in which all minds are given to the hands of Christ, to be returned to spirit in the name of true creation and the Will of God. The Second Coming is the one event in time which time itself can not affect. For every one who ever came to die, or yet will come or who is present now, is equally released from what he made. In this equality is Christ restored as one Identity, in which the Sons of God acknowledge that they all are one. And God the Father smiles upon His Son, His one creation and His only joy."* [273]

There are indeed many more huge differences between Christianity and the teachings of *ACIM*, including the concepts of sin, Atonement, the Last Judgement, the Crucifixion, the Resurrection and the Second Coming (mentioned above), to name but a few. But the overall messages of both the Bible and *ACIM* are not that dissimilar. Both teachings emphasise *love* and *forgiveness* as the way to eternal bliss (even though the concept of forgiveness in *ACIM* differs considerably from the traditional concept of forgiveness that we find in the Bible.) There is neither a single word nor a single sentence in *ACIM* that in any way supports hate, judgement, violence, war, retribution or revenge. The focus of the Text, Workbook and Manual is on forgiveness and love. And that's one of the things I love about the *Course*. The only radical thing about *ACIM* is that it is trying to explain to us that all we see with our eyes is simply not real. God did *not* create the human body or personality or the universe. He created spirit, and everything else is just an illusion. The way to return to Heaven is to practise forgiveness at every step of the way; towards whomever one comes across and in whatever situation or circumstance that presents itself to us. And if everyone on this planet did that, we would be living in paradise on earth! So, if both *ACIM* and Christianity have love and forgiveness at their core, does it make any sense

---

[273] *ACIM*, W449.

to focus on the differences? And do the differences really matter? If the differences do seem to matter, I think it is true to say that they are only of concern *to the ego*. To those who are keen to overcome the grip of the ego and return to Source, only love and forgiveness matter.

But *why* is forgiveness so important and is at the heart of the teachings of the *Course?* First and foremost is the fact that this life we are living is as real as a dream. The ego made it up and so whatever seems to happen here *is not really happening at all*. This may seem hard to believe because everything seems so real and so tangible. But in dreams things seem equally real, *until you wake up.* *"Salvation is a paradox indeed! What could it be except a happy dream? It asks you but that you forgive all things that no one ever did; to overlook what is not there, and not to look upon the unreal as reality."* [274] And further on the Text explains that anger is never justified but forgiveness is always justified.*"Pardon is **always** justified. It has a sure foundation. You do not forgive the unforgivable, nor overlook a real attack that calls for punishment. Salvation does not lie in being asked to make unnatural responses which are inappropriate to what is real. Instead, it merely asks that you respond appropriately to what is not real by not perceiving what has not occurred."* [275]   Not perceiving what has not occurred! This means when things happen to upset us, we must pay no attention to them because they didn't really occur. This has been called *advanced forgiveness* or *quantum forgiveness* by a number of people who have written books on the subject. So the *Course* asks us to forgive all the people around us because they are only really figures in a dream.

The second reason why we should forgive is that, as we are all one, joined at the level of the mind, if we don't forgive another person, then we are not forgiving ourselves. Similarly if we judge others, we are also judging ourselves. The *Course* tells us that what we see around us is simply one ego, appearing as many. In reality there isn't even that one ego. All that exists is spirit, and all the extensions of Christ's spirit are connected to each other, to Christ and to God. How then can we judge or condemn another? *"You and your brother are the same, as God Himself is One and not divided in His Will. And you must have one purpose,*

---

[274] *ACIM,* T635.
[275] *ACIM,* T638.

since He gave the same to both of you. His Will is brought together as you join in will, that you be made complete by offering completion to your brother. See not in him the sinfulness he sees, but give him honor that you may esteem yourself and him." [276]

This following passage, which I have referred to earlier, explains just why forgiveness is so important. *"Look once again upon your brother, not without the understanding that he is the way to Heaven or to hell, as you perceive him. But forget not this; the role you give to him is given you, and you will walk the way you pointed out to him because it is your judgment on yourself."* [277] This means that if we forgive others we can make it out of here and get back Home. If we don't, we are doomed to living a life of illusion here on earth (hell.) Whatever we give, we receive. If we give forgiveness it will come back to us in some way. It may appear that we are forgiving all the time and others simply take advantage of us and do not respond in kind. But it is explained in *ACIM* that if the other person is not willing to accept your forgiveness, the Holy Spirit will keep it for him (store it away somewhere) and give it to him when he is ready to accept it. So no forgiveness is ever "wasted."

Another aspect to forgiveness is that it has a healing effect on those who practice it because it gives them peace. *"How willing are you to forgive your brother? How much do you desire peace instead of endless strife and misery and pain? These questions are the same, in different form. Forgiveness is your peace, for herein lies the end of separation and the dream of danger and destruction, sin and death; of madness and of murder; grief and loss. This is the 'sacrifice' salvation asks, and gladly offers peace instead of this."* [278]

It is no good going around telling everyone you forgive them if you still harbour a grudge against them; or if you are just saying it because you think you should; or because you feel upset about what they did but are going to overlook it. *"Forgiveness is an empty gesture unless it entails correction. Without this it is essentially judgemental, rather than healing."* [279] This means that forgiveness has to

---

[276] *ACIM*, T523.

[277] *ACIM*, T529.

[278] *ACIM*, T615 & 616.

[279] *ACIM*, T28.

be based on a changed perception of the world or recognition of the fact that nothing really happened that warrants forgiveness. It's not a matter of saying "I'll forgive you for what you did," but rather of realising that there is nothing to forgive because it's all an illusion.

There is yet another aspect of forgiveness and it is linked to the concept of projection. The ego projects all its negative feelings onto others so, when people appear negative and unpleasant to us, it would be wise to remember that their negative words or deeds could very well have emanated from our own egos. Furthermore, it is a possibility that, at some level, we put a particularly irritating individual into our lives in order to give us opportunities to practise forgiveness. So these people could be considered to be our teachers in a way. Therefore, there is not much point in reacting to them because that would simply mean that we have refused to learn the lessons *we wanted them to teach us*. I know that sounds a bit implausible but it helps to keep an open mind.

Whilst re-reading the preface of *ACIM* I came across yet another significant aspect of forgiveness that I would like to share with the reader. *"Through forgiveness the thinking of the world is reversed. The forgiven world becomes the gate of Heaven, because by its mercy we can at last forgive ourselves. Holding no one prisoner to guilt, we become free. Acknowledging Christ in all our brothers, we recognize His Presence in ourselves. Forgetting all our misperceptions, and with nothing from the past to hold us back, we can remember God."* [280] So by forgiving we overcome the huge amount of guilt in our subconscious minds and in doing so we set ourselves free. We cast away all the illusions or misperceptions about the world and then there is nothing to keep us trapped in time. Finally we achieve liberation and *"remember God."*

It's easy to understand all these different facets of forgiveness and then when something really annoying happens to you, it's just as easy to forget it all and get upset or take offence. I know from my own experience. But we are asked to remember our inner strength (which is derived from the fact that we are one with God) and to remember that illusions cannot hurt us in any way, even though it may appear otherwise. *"It is not you who are so vulnerable and open to*

---

[280] *ACIM,* Preface xiii.

attack that just a little word, a little whisper that you do not like, a circumstance that suits you not, or an event that you did not anticipate upsets your world, and hurls it into chaos. Truth is not frail. Illusions leave it perfectly unmoved and undisturbed." [281] So if we are to be miracle-workers and change our perception of the world because we know it's all an illusion, then we have to remember that we are not vulnerable and that we can rise above the small (or large) irritations of daily life. And whenever I get upset I stop myself and repeat Lesson 121, *"Forgiveness is the key to happiness"*; or Lesson 62, *"Forgiveness is my function as the light of the world"*; or Lesson 333, *"Forgiveness ends the dream of conflict here."* This last lesson highlights the fact that it's all a dream. In fact, it is a collective dream that we are all sharing because we are all joined together. Lesson 62 makes me feel good because it is such a nice thought to see oneself as the light of the world. And Lesson 121 is an uplifting statement. Who wouldn't want the key to happiness? But forgiveness is not an easy process and it requires constant vigilance and hard work. Also, it can be difficult to remember to forgive others because we are all joined together as one, due to the simple reason that we all appear to be separate individuals or separate bodies. That's why the *Course* keeps reminding us that we are not bodies. So sometimes when my mother says something irritating, I remind myself that she is really part of me and what appears to irritate me is only her ego, irritating my ego. I also tell myself that the Holy Spirit would never be irritated by her, so I shouldn't be!

The Holy Spirit has a plan of forgiveness, which is referred to as Atonement. It simply involves remembering that anything upsetting is unreal and therefore should be ignored. One wouldn't, after all, take offense at a figure in a dream. The situation in our waking hours is just the same. *"Forgiveness through the Holy Spirit lies simply in looking beyond error from the beginning, and thus keeping it unreal for you...what has no effect does not exist, and to the Holy Spirit the effects of error are nonexistent."* [282]

So whenever I become upset I remind myself that it hasn't really happened. At first it was difficult to do this, but with practice it has become easier. It doesn't

---

[281] *ACIM,* T506.
[282] *ACIM,* T169.

mean that irritating people or circumstances don't affect me, but nowadays it is easier to let them go and stand back and observe it all, aware that I might have created all these characters and events in my life for some reason. Maybe so that I could practice my forgiveness lessons and awaken from the dream. Yes, I created my surly boss at work, my office with no external window, which I refer to as my "dungeon," and the over-crowded conditions, which are quite aggravating at times. I must have put them all into my life for a reason. So it seems pretty pointless getting annoyed by them.

What is the holy instant? It involves choosing the perspective of the Holy Spirit, whenever a situation arises that has the potential to upset your peace of mind. This means not defending yourself, not attacking another and not reacting in any way because those are the ways that the ego responds to situations. And one has to constantly remember that there are only two ways of doing things: the ego's way or the Holy Spirit's way. By choosing the holy instant and giving it to others (through forgiveness) we actually receive it ourselves. *"The Holy Spirit gives their blessed instant to you through your giving it. As you give it, He offers it to you. Be not unwilling to give what you would receive of Him, for you join with Him in giving...How long is an instant? As long as it takes to re-establish perfect sanity, perfect peace and perfect love for everyone, for God and for yourself."* [283] So by choosing the holy instant it seems obvious that everyone will benefit. Perfect peace and perfect love sound wonderful but the difficulty is that we have been listening to the ego for so long, that we have to work quite hard at ignoring its clamorous demands and following the Holy Spirit instead.

Choosing forgiveness has a massive payback; it releases us from time. We saw in Chapter 6 how we are trapped by the ego in the illusion of time and space and in particular trapped by the past that keeps repeating itself over and over because we can't let go of it. If we choose to forgive others we are able to free ourselves from this trap. *"Forgiveness is the great release from time. It is the key to learning that the past is over. Madness speaks no more. There **is** no other teacher and no other way. For what has been undone no longer is....And do you want that fearful instant kept, when Heaven seemed to disappear and God was feared and made a symbol of your*

---

283 *ACIM*, T304.

hate? Forget the time of terror that has been so long ago corrected and undone...." [284] The last two sentences remind us that all our problems stem from the moment of separation when we appeared to abandon God and Heaven. All our fear and mistrust of others stems from this moment through the process of projection by the ego.

Author Gary Renard explains, in his book *Your Immortal Reality*, that by forgiving others we speed up the process of enlightenment because the Holy Spirit will step in and assist us. *"Because of your practice of forgiveness, there are lessons that you no longer need to learn, and the Holy Spirit is actually erasing the tapes, taking dimensions of time that held lessons you would have needed to learn if you didn't practice forgiveness, and making those dimensions disappear...More layers of the onion have been peeled away, and your ego is vanishing."* [285] That is a really encouraging thought.

Gary Renard gave a lively and thought-provoking workshop in London recently. He pointed out that the ego will actually try to give you bad memories, which is why it is so important to stamp them out whenever you can. He also said something very significant about the lessons in the Workbook of *ACIM*. He said that all the lessons are inter-related and each lesson is holographic, i.e., each lesson contains the whole teaching of the *Course*. Therefore, if you remember only one lesson you have, in fact, remembered all. I thought that was amazing and very motivating because, out of the 365 lessons, I think I can only really consciously remember and recite about 40. However, if those 40 lessons give me access to the *whole teaching*, then that is quite something. The reason I remember these particular 40 lessons is that, having completed the *Course*, I have written down the 40 most significant lessons for me and I continue to carry one around with me every day so as to focus on it. Every 40 days I go back to the first of those lessons and repeat the whole process again. I do plan, however, to go through the whole Workbook again, at some point. I have noticed that each time I re-read passages of the *Course*, I learn something new. It could be that certain things had not really "sunk in", when I first read them, but now they do. In any

---

[284] *ACIM*, T551.
[285] Gary Renard *Your Immortal Reality*, p. 75, Hay House Inc., Carlsbad, CA, 2006.

case, I believe that it would take at least a lifetime of study to really understand the *Course* properly.

To return to the subject of forgiveness again, the reason why we find it so difficult is because we believe that there really are things that we have to forgive. In other words we don't realise that it's all an illusion. So when something horrible happens we find it hard to forgive the perpetrator because we believe that it really happened, when, in fact, it didn't. *"The major difficulty that you find in genuine forgiveness on your part is that you still believe you must forgive the truth and not illusions. You conceive of pardon as a vain attempt to look past what is there; to overlook the truth, in an unfounded effort to deceive yourself by making an illusion true."* [286] In one way it is understandable because things do appear to be so real to us. When we watch, for example, a deranged person going into a shopping mall and shooting people at random, *it does seem real*. That is why it is so important to realise that *it isn't*. And when we realise that it isn't, it becomes easier to forgive. A part of me, however, would really struggle with forgiveness if one of my nearest and dearest happened to have been shot in that shopping mall. It would take a huge amount of inner work and calling upon the Holy Spirit to come to terms with that, I know. Yet that is what Jesus is asking us to do. But maybe it is not as enormous a task as it appears because I think there is a cumulative effect to forgiveness. If we start forgiving the little things, then more and more of them, perhaps one day we will find it easier to forgive bigger things.

Forgiving *oneself* is just as important as forgiving others. We need to be forgiving towards ourselves because of all the guilt we carry around with us due to the original (illusory) act of separation. By projecting guilt onto others or by holding onto it ourselves, we harm ourselves and others and one of the results is ill health. The *Course* also teaches us that defensiveness is to be avoided. We should never feel the need to be defensive. I recall these words whenever I feel tempted to stick up for myself. *"Forget not, when you feel the need arise to be defensive about anything, you have identified yourself with an illusion. And therefore feel that you are weak because you are alone. This is the cost of all illusions."* [287] So now I

---

[286] *ACIM*, W 248, Lesson 134.
[287] *ACIM*, W480.

just shrug my shoulders and don't bother to explain why I did or did not do something. It's all an illusion anyway; so why bother? If I do stop and defend myself, I now know that it is merely my ego reacting to the ego of another person. Egos need to be ignored and not reacted to. But, like everything in the *Course*, it takes a lot of practice to remember not to defend yourself.

Taking ownership of one's negative thoughts and emotions and refusing to see oneself as a victim have a vital role in the forgiveness process. Author Ken Wilber, about whom I have spoken before, explains that if we firstly accept that the negative emotions and thoughts we have projected onto others and into the environment are actually coming from ourselves, then we are free to stop the process. We are free to choose not to feel angry, depressed, sad, guilty, etc. and not to hate or blame others. It is through this process that we get rid of the split in the ego (Ken Wilber calls this the split between the persona and Shadow, the latter being the projected facets of the ego) and, "*...in this fashion I spontaneously evolve an accurate and therefore acceptable unitary self-image, that is to say, an accurate mental representation of my entire psychosomatic organism. Thus is my psyche integrated....*" [288] In other words, through taking responsibility for our own negative tendencies and refusing to blame or judge others, we heal ourselves and become whole. This is exactly what *A Course in Miracles* teaches, emphasising that it is through taking responsibility for our ego's projections and through forgiveness that we heal the "split" mind.

I recently took myself off to southern Spain for a short holiday to get some sunshine. It was a wonderful break and a time to sit quietly by myself and think. How, I asked myself, could I devote more of my life to the Holy Spirit? Then it dawned on me, as I was gazing out across the rooftops, attractive palm trees and the shimmering blue Mediterranean Sea, that simply by forgiving, in my mind, everyone and everything that bothers me on a daily basis, I *am* serving the Holy Spirit. It's so simple. By choosing forgiveness, I am using my "right" mind, which is the part of the mind where the Holy Spirit dwells. So I don't really need to go out and try to change the world. All I need to do is to change how I *perceive*

---

[288] Ken Wilber, *The Spectrum of Consciousness*, p. 222, Quest Books, The Theosophical Publishing House, Illinois, USA, 1985, www.questbooks.net.

everything in my little world and in the world at large. By perceiving everything in a loving and forgiving manner, I am serving God. Why, I wondered, did it take me so long to understand? Now I finally realise that I can serve God every day whilst still in my existing job, home, etc. My outer circumstances don't have to change but my perception definitely does. Furthermore, it is good to remember that forgiveness leads to liberation, which is the goal of life.

Apart from the fact that forgiveness eventually leads to enlightenment, the everyday benefits that come from being forgiving are numerous. Being unforgiving, judgemental and having a hard heart can't be a good way of living one's life. This way of thinking has to be a heavy burden to carry around all day. It is not the way that leads to happiness and joy and I think it must take a huge amount of one's energy to maintain this attitude all day and every day. Tai Chi teacher and healer, Jason Chan, stresses the importance of forgiveness in his inspiring little book, entitled *Seven Principles for Radiant Living.* I attended one of his workshops in London recently and he did seem to exude an air of peacefulness and radiance. In his book he said, *"Forgiveness is vital in the letting go process....Gradually as you learn the art of letting go, you will be amazed at how your relationships blossom. Jealousy, guilt and insecurity will dissipate as you let go of your past hurts and imagination. You will become whole and cease to need too much from others. Instead of imprisoning your loved ones with your fears, you will allow them to be whole too, and you will learn to fly together."* [289]

Adversity will decline in our lives when we practice forgiveness and thereby release the ego. Those were the words of Nouk Sanchez and Tomas Vieira, whose workshop I referred to earlier in this book. They pointed out that we have to remember that there is really only one ego *appearing as many*; so we forgive others because we realise that there is nobody else out there. We are all one.

Nouk Sanchez and Tomas Vieira also said something that I thought was quite significant. They said we must laugh at ourselves because, if we can't do this, it means we are taking this "dream" too seriously. I think we all take life too seriously because it's the only "reality" we know about. Raising children and giving them the best education, having a good career and earning lots of money

---

[289] Jason Chan, *Seven Principles for Radiant Living,* Chapter 2, Light Foundation, Manchester, 2002.

are all things we take very seriously. And whilst it is important to raise children well, so that they are happy and well-adjusted, I don't think *what* they do with their lives is all that important, provided they continue to be happy and well-adjusted. One has to ask oneself if a university degree is really that important given that this world is just a dream. Does it really matter what career path one goes down, provided one is peaceful and contented in life and one does not harm others in any way? I can't see that it does. In fact, there's a long list of things that seemed to matter to me or to be of interest to me in the past, but that are no longer all that relevant. Since I have come to the realisation that we are as real as figures in a dream, things like politics, economics, science and history, to name but a few, all seem to have lost their relevance to me. How can they really matter when the world is unreal and all of us are just images of our true reality (spirit)?

As *ACIM* is a course on forgiveness, it may seem strange to realise that forgiveness itself is part of the illusion. The *Course* teaches us, however, that this illusion is the only one that doesn't propagate other illusions because it is part of the awakening process. *"Forgiveness sweeps all other dreams away, and though it is itself a dream, it breeds no others. All illusions save this one must multiply a thousandfold. But this is where illusions end...Forgiveness is the only road that leads out of disaster, past all suffering, and finally away from death. How could there be another way, when this one is the plan of God Himself?"* [290] This last sentence illustrates just how important forgiveness really is. It is part of God's plan! When we have learnt all our forgiveness lessons and returned to Source, we will have no further use for forgiveness because in Heaven there is nothing and no one to forgive. We have returned to our original state of oneness with God, Christ and His extensions (which, in fact, we never actually left but thought we did.)

Browsing through the Buddhist scripture, the *Dhammapada*, one day, I came across several verses that related to forgiveness. Here are a few of them:

"Let us live happily then, not hating those who hate us! Among men
who hate us let us dwell free from hatred!
Let a man overcome anger by love, let him overcome evil by good, let
him overcome the greedy by liberality, the liar by truth!

---

[290] *ACIM*, W 379, Lesson 198.

No one should attack a Brahmana, [291] but no Brahmana if attacked
should let himself fly at his aggressor! Woe to him who strikes a
Brahmana, more woe to him who flies at his aggressor!
Him I call indeed a Brahmana who finds no fault with other beings,
whether feeble or strong, and does not kill nor cause slaughter.
Him I call indeed a Brahmana who utters true speech, instructive and
free from harshness, so that he offend no one" [292]

As I approach the end of this chapter I would like to take a brief look at some of the numerous lessons in *ACIM* that deal with forgiveness. Readers who would like to pursue the topic of forgiveness are advised to read the whole lesson in each case. *"I could see peace instead of this....Love holds no grievances....My grievances hide the light of the world in me...Holding grievances is an attack on God's plan for salvation....Let miracles replace all grievances....Forgiveness offers everything I want." [293]*

The following passage explains the dynamics of forgiveness and shows how beneficial forgiveness is to the one who practices it. *"The strength of pardon is its honesty, which is so uncorrupted that it sees illusions as illusions, not as truth....By its ability to overlook what is not there, it opens up the way to truth, which has been blocked by dreams of guilt. Now are you free to follow in the way your true forgiveness opens up to you. For if one brother has received this gift of you, the door is open to yourself." [294]*

Let me end with what I call, "*ACIM* in a nutshell": *"Forgive the world, and you will understand that everything that God created cannot have an end, and nothing He did not create is real. In this one sentence is our Course explained. In this one sentence is our practicing given its one direction. And in this one sentence is the Holy Spirit's whole curriculum specified exactly as it is." [295]*

---

[291] A *Brahmana* here refers to a spiritual practitioner.

[292] *Dhammapada – A Collection of Verses from the Pali Canon of Buddhism,* Verses 197, 223, 389, 405 & 408, translated by F Max Muller, Red & Black Publishers, Florida, 2008.

[293] *ACIM,* Workbook Lessons 34, 68, 69, 72, 78 & 122.

[294] *ACIM,* W 249, Lesson 134.

[295] *ACIM,* M 52.

Chapter 10

The Inevitability of Enlightenment

"Blessed is he who has found enlightenment." [296]

If you become aware that life on earth is all an illusion, eventually the world and all its pleasures may leave a rather bitter taste in your mouth. When you realise that all the good times and all the bad times didn't really mean that much because they only happened within the illusion, then the world gradually begins to lose its appeal. So one starts to look elsewhere and this does not entail any sacrifice, contrary to what some may believe. In fact, one begins to develop a sense of longing for what is true and what is real, i.e., for God and heaven. The futility of running after transient pleasures becomes more and more apparent, and so there is no sense of loss when one turns one's back, to a certain extent, on the world of form. In fact, the longer we're stuck here, the greater the loss. I used the words "to a certain extent" because, as long as we are living here, there will be things we have to do and there will still be things that bring pleasure and pain.

If turning away from things of the world does seem like sacrifice, then all that means is that one has not yet become satiated and perhaps enjoying the many pleasures of the world of form *is* the right thing to do, *for the present moment.* Sooner or later though we will all awaken from the dream and we will all want to. I am convinced of that.

---

[296] *The Gospel of the Buddha, Chapter 4, Truth, The Savior,* compiled from Ancient Records by Paul Carus 1909, www.sacred-texts.com/bud.

If I choose to ignore the fact that the world and everything in it is an illusion, I would be like an ostrich burying its head in the sand. I just know that eventually we will all have to wake up from our dreams of life on earth. And now that I know they are actually meaningless and non-existent, I have been greatly encouraged to get a move on! The *Course* tells us that Christ is asking us all to, *"Choose once again, if you would take your place among the saviours of the world, or would remain in hell, and hold your brothers there."* [297] Who, in their right mind, would choose to remain in hell? The trouble is that many of us don't realise that we are stuck in hell here on earth. But once you become aware of the illusory and repetitive nature of physical plane existence, then you do realise how trapped you are. And for me, freedom has always been a motivating factor in all aspects of my life.

Before I became an *ACIM* student I thought enlightenment was something that I would eventually attain several lifetimes from now (with more than a bit of luck.) But now that I am aware of the fact that it's all an illusion, this has given me a huge impetus and motivation. I am really happy that I can at last begin to consciously awaken from a dream I didn't even know I was dreaming. Now I can actually begin to consider becoming enlightened, dare I say, in the not too distant future? Can I do this in my present lifetime or, at the very most, in a few more lifetimes? This now seems a possibility thanks to the teachings of Jesus in *ACIM*. I know I have a great deal of hard work to do and much personal transformation to accomplish and it could still take me a very long while to ascend. But I give thanks to God every day for having been led to the *Course*, through His grace. I know there are other paths to God but I have finally found one path that suits me.

Meditation plays an important role in the awakening process but I don't think meditation alone is my path. Maybe this is because meditation has been rather difficult for me. I have meditated every day for nearly 25 years, but it has often been a battle to quieten my overactive mind. However, there have been days when I have seen a glimmer of light above the chatter of my mind and days when I have clearly heard spoken phrases. In addition, meditation is extremely

---

[297] *ACIM*, T666.

relaxing and it turns one's attention away from mundane life, so it is very beneficial. I know that some people have achieved enlightenment through meditation and it is a path followed by both Buddhists and Hindus, but I have not felt that meditation alone will take me back Home. Yet it is a practice I would not do without.

Enlightenment will eventually involve leaving the world of the ego completely behind and moving on without it. This inevitably must appear to be very threatening and frightening to the ego, because extinction is not a pleasant thought. I think this is why my ego often resists the process. Sometimes a sudden flash of fear engulfs my mind, usually last thing at night or at the unearthly hour of 3 or 4 a.m. I awaken almost trembling with fear and at first I could not understand it. Then one day I realised that it was the doings of the ego, yet again. Insisting on clinging on and fearful for its own survival, it breeds anxiety and even panic in my mind. When this happens I call upon the Holy Spirit for help and ask Him to turn my thoughts to right-mindedness. If that doesn't work I get up and make myself a hot herbal drink!

We are told that enlightenment does not involve extinction of anything but the ego. If we look at the term *nirvana*, it stands for liberation or spiritual perfection. But it does not involve annihilation. In an online encyclopaedia of religion I came across the following: *"There is a wrong interpretation of the term Nirvana—as one's disappearance in the emptiness (void.) No: it is one's lower self that disappears in the emptiness, but one's Higher Self merges into the Ocean of the Universal Primordial Consciousness, enriching It by this."* [298]

ACIM states something similar. With reference to the time when all egos have become one and the physical world is no more, it says, *"The end of the world is not its destruction, but its translation into Heaven."* [299]

An interesting debate about the self and about nirvana can be found in a book that I have mentioned before, *The Monk and The Philosopher*. Jean-Francois Revel (the Buddhist monk) explains to his father (the philosopher) that upon attainment of nirvana, the self is not abolished because it is non-existent. *"A non-*

[298] www.encyclopedia-of-religion.org/nirvana.
[299] *ACIM*, T 211.

existent self can't really be 'abolished,' but its non-existence can be recognized. What we want to abolish is the illusion, the mistake that has no inherent existence in the first place...So nirvana isn't the extinction of anything, but the final knowledge of the nature of things..." [300]

That great thinker Wei Wu Wei dealt with topic of the non-existence of the self in a number of his books. With reference to the issue of how a person can be expected to believe that he does not exist, he explained that there is no such identity as that person in the first place. But what he can do is to *become aware* that he is not what he appears to be phenomenally. In other words, we need to change our awareness or perception of the phenomenal world, including ourselves. This is tantamount to what was said in the previous paragraph, i.e., we need to have true knowledge of the nature of things as they really are and of the non-existence of the self, or in the terminology of *ACIM*, we need to *awaken from the dream.*

As we rush around everyday getting all our work and chores done, it is good sometimes to slow down and stop and remind oneself that there is more to life than our mundane existence. There is another goal. *"Let me remember that my goal is God,"* states Lesson 258 and it continues, *"All that is needful is to train our minds to overlook all little senseless aims, and to remember that our goal is God. His memory is hidden in our minds, obscured but by our pointless little goals which offer nothing, and do not exist."* [301] What are our pointless little, non-existent goals? Paying the mortgage, preparing food, raising the children, having a career, going on holiday, going out, buying clothes, etc., most of which are really necessary and don't seem pointless at all. In terms of survival of the body they are not pointless. But Jesus is only concerned with our salvation and our return to our original nature—spirit. Putting God ahead of these activities would require quite a radical change in perspective because all these things are ingrained habits we have acquired. God-realisation therefore has to be cultivated as a new habit, at least for us in the West where prayer, visiting temples, sitting with gurus and

---

[300] Jean-François Revel & Mathieu Ricard, *The Monk and The Philosopher*, pp. 34-35, Thorsons, HarperCollins Publishers, London, Random House, Inc., NY, © 1998 by Jean-François Revel & Mathieu Ricard.

[301] *ACIM*, W 423, Lesson 258.

meditating are usually not part of our normal daily routine. But I believe we *can* combine our usual daily activities with certain spiritual practices. It is just a matter of adapting one's lifestyle a little and making time for things such as meditation, reading scriptures or spiritual teachings, awakening from the dream and remembering to practice forgiveness and compassion.

"The sole object of life is the attainment of Self-realisation or absolute freedom. The aim of man's life is to unfold and manifest the Godhead which is eternally existent within him. The purpose of life is to lose all sense of distinctive personality and be dissolved in the Lord. The attainment of the Infinite Life is the supreme purpose of finite life." [302] These were the words of the renowned Indian guru, Swami Sivananda. I believe, however, that it's no use telling anyone that Self-realisation or God-realisation is the only goal of life, as it is something one has to discover for oneself. If someone had told me that years ago, I would probably have nodded my head but thought that it did not apply to me because I was too busy enjoying life. It has taken years of reading, searching for meaning and personal transformation work for me to reach a stage in my life where I can now wholeheartedly agree with Swami Sivananda and make Self-realisation my own personal goal.

Enlightenment or awakening from the dream is at the crux of the teachings of both Buddhism and Hinduism. It is also referred to as self-realisation and overcoming ignorance. This is because it is only due to ignorance that we identify with the ego or lower self and when we awaken we become aware of our true nature, which is spirit or immortal self. *"This world is like a dream, crowded with loves and hates; in its own time it shines like a reality; but on awakening it becomes unreal."* [303]

The Christian Scientist, Joel Goldsmith dealt at length with the topic of spiritual growth and personal transformation and, as I have mentioned before, he advised his students to turn away from the things of this world because of their unreal nature. *"You can measure your acceptance of the spiritual teaching by the*

---

[302] Swami Sivananda, *Bliss Divine – A Book of Spiritual Essays on the Lofty Purpose of Human Life and the Means to its Achievement*, pp. 300-301, compiled by Sri Ananthanarayanan, The Divine Life Society, Himalayas, India, 2006.

[303] Charles Johnston, *The Crest-Jewel of Wisdom and other writings of Śankarâchârya, The Awakening to the Self, www.sacred-texts.com/hin/cjw/cjw16.htm.*

degree of concern that you are losing about personal welfare. You must come to that place in consciousness where you live by grace, where you attain a measure of the Christ and can always find yourself in the same relative condition of harmonious life regardless of any human changes that take place politically or economically." [304] That's an interesting gauge of one's spiritual progress. It must be quite an achievement to have perfect harmony in one's life all the time, regardless of what destiny dishes out.

The *Course* says that Atonement (the process of changing one's perception and following the Holy Spirit's teaching on forgiveness) leads to a re-evaluation of all that was once dear to us because it separates the true from the false. This will entail accepting our own guiltlessness and that of others. If we recognise that we are holy, as the *Course* teaches, then we will not project guilt onto others. *"Eternal holiness abides in me."* [305] If we are holy, we should not feel guilty for anything. We feel guilty because of the original separation but if we remember that *it never really happened,* then there is no need to feel any guilt at all. We are advised to, *"Release from guilt as you would be released. There is no other way to look within and see the light of love, shining as steadily and as surely as God Himself has always loved His Son. And as His Son loves Him..."* [306]

The Zen teacher, the Bodhidharma, stressed that one has to have a spiritual teacher if one is to make spiritual progress. *"If you don't find a teacher soon, you'll live this life in vain. It's true, you have the Buddha-nature. But without the help of a teacher you'll never know it. Only one person in a million becomes enlightened without a teacher's help."* [307] And Sri Ramana Maharishi also said that a guru was needed to guide disciples along the Path. *"Knowing intellectually about the nature of the Self, one should stop there. Intellectual knowledge has to be transformed into intuitive awareness. For this, the spark of the Guru's Grace, which is nothing other than Divine Intervention, is required..."* [308] But Ramana Maharishi said the guru need not be in

---

[304] Joel S Goldsmith, *Spiritual Interpretation of Scripture,* p. 92, Willing Publishing Company, San Gabriel, California, 1969.

[305] *ACIM,* W448, Lesson 299.

[306] *ACIM,* T265.

[307] Red Pine, *The Zen Teaching of Bodhidharma,* p. 15, North Point Press, New York, 1989.

[308] Nagesh D. Sonde, *Philosophy of Bhagavan Sri Ramana Maharishi,* p. 45, Sri Satguru Publications, Delhi, 2005.

human form.

ACIM also emphasises that a teacher is needed—the Holy Spirit. At each moment of our lives we make decisions and choices. The *Course* teaches us that there are really only two, mutually exclusive choices: listening to the ego or to the Holy Spirit. Each time we overlook something that upsets us, or forgive or refuse to take offence at a perceived attack by another person, we are choosing to listen to the Holy Spirit. These are *"holy instants."* Each time we get upset, hurt, angry, sad, dejected, etc., we are letting the ego rule us and we are stuck. It would appear in theory to be an easy choice to make, but in practice it often isn't. One would have to be almost saintly to never get annoyed or irritated. One has to consciously work at it and remember at all times to call upon the Holy Spirit for guidance. *"In order to heal, it thus becomes essential for the teacher of God to let all his own mistakes be corrected. If he senses even the faintest hint of irritation in himself as he responds to anyone, let him instantly realize that he has made an interpretation that is not true. Then let him turn within to his eternal Guide, and let Him judge what the response should be. So is he healed, and in his healing is his pupil healed."* [309] And Jesus tells us that we *can* do this and it is one of the fastest ways Home.

Course teacher, Kenneth Wapnick, explains that we won't all hear the voice of the Holy Spirit as a spoken voice. There are other ways that He will get His message through to us, such as through the words of a friend, or a dream or a flash of intuition. I would imagine though that having an open mind would be a necessary prerequisite. But I am sure that if anyone calls upon the Holy Spirit, He will reply in one way or another, even if the reply does not come immediately.

What makes the teachings of *ACIM* very special, in my opinion, is that they are positive, uplifting, encouraging and motivating. There is no emphasis on sin, suffering, sacrifice, renunciation or difficult thought-stopping meditation. All we are asked to give up is illusions—the unreal. Lesson 322 states, *"I can give up but what was never real"* and it goes on to explain that we sacrifice illusions and only illusions. *"And as illusions go I find the gifts illusions tried to hide, awaiting me in*

---

[309] *ACIM*, M48.

shining welcome, and in readiness to give God's ancient message to me." [310] And in the Text we read, *"There is no need to learn through pain. And gentle lessons are acquired joyously, and are remembered gladly. What gives you happiness you want to learn and not forget....?"* [311]

It is made quite clear in the *Course*, however, that until we give up our belief in the body as being something real, we will not achieve salvation. We are told in Lesson 100, *"Salvation must reverse the mad belief in separate thoughts and separate bodies, which lead separate lives and go their separate ways. One function shared by separate minds unites them in one purpose, for each of them is equally essential to them all."* Then it is explained that each one of us is essential to God's plan and that we should be joyous because, *"Without your joy, His joy is incomplete. Without your smile, the world cannot be saved...Sadness is the sign that you would play another part, instead of what has been assigned to you by God...You have indeed been wrong in your belief that sacrifice is asked. You but receive according to God's plan, and never lose or sacrifice or die."* [312] I really like this part of the *Course* and find it to be so inspiring. God's plan is for us to remember that we have never really separated from Him and that we are all joined as part of the one Sonship. It means that we have to awaken from the dream, realise that everything around us is simply an illusion, and follow the advice of God's Ambassador, the Holy Spirit, so as to return Home. And we should be joyful whilst we are doing this.

The *Course* has this to say about different methods of attaining salvation. *"It is extremely difficult to teach Atonement by fighting against sin. Enormous effort is expended in the attempt to make holy what is hated and despised. Nor is a lifetime of contemplation and long periods of meditation aimed at detachment from the body necessary. All such attempts will ultimately succeed because of their purpose. Yet the means are tedious and very time consuming, for all of them look to the future for release from a state of present unworthiness and inadequacy. Your way will be different, not in purpose but in means. A holy relationship is a means of saving time. One instant spent together with your brother restores the universe to both of you. You are prepared. Now you need but to remember you need do nothing...'I need do nothing' is a statement of*

---

[310] *ACIM*, W 462, Lesson 322.
[311] *ACIM*, T446.
[312] *ACIM*, T180 & 181.

allegiance, a truly undivided loyalty. Believe it for just one instant, and you will accomplish more than is given to a century of contemplation, or of struggle against temptation." [313]

The statement *"I need do nothing"* doesn't mean one can become a couch potato, put one's legs up and do nothing at all. It means to withdraw one's focus from the body and from all that has gone by in the past and simply be still and listen to the guidance of the Holy Spirit. This, we are told, could save us *centuries* of hard slogging. *"Here is the quick and open door through which you slip past centuries of effort, and escape from time. This is the way in which sin loses all attraction right now. For here is time denied, and past and future gone...To do nothing is to rest, and make a place within you where the activity of the body ceases to demand attention. Into this place the Holy Spirit comes, and there abides. He will remain when you forget, and the body's activities return to occupy your conscious mind."* [314] Then it is explained that if we develop the ability to be still and listen to the Holy Spirit, we will improve at this until eventually, *"This quiet center, in which you do nothing, will remain with you, giving you rest in the midst of every busy doing on which you are sent."*

Although *ACIM* states that long periods of meditation are not necessary, several lessons refer to the need to remain still and quiet so as to hear the Holy Spirit. In fact, if one is busy rushing around all the time, I don't think it is possible to ignore the activities of the body and welcome in the Holy Spirit. Lesson 106 says, *"Let me be still and listen to the truth."* We are urged to be quiet and listen to the Voice for God—the Holy Spirit, whose function is to bring about our salvation. *"Listen, and hear your Father speak to you through His appointed Voice, which silences the thunder of the meaningless, and shows the way to peace to those who cannot see. Be still today and listen to the truth."* [315] Other lessons in the Workbook also deal with stillness: Lesson 273, *"The stillness of the peace of God is mine"*; Lesson 125, *"In quiet I receive God's Word today"*; Lesson 254, *"Let every voice but God's be still in me"*; and Lesson 255, *"This day I choose to spend in perfect peace."*

---

[313] *ACIM*, T389 & 390.
[314] *ACIM*, T390.
[315] *ACIM*, W190, Lesson 106.

Actually, the following passage is, in a way, suggesting that one should meditate. *"In stillness we will hear God's Voice today without intrusion of our petty thoughts, without our personal desires, and without all judgment of His holy Word...Today we will not listen to the world, but wait in silence for the Word of God."* [316] And this is what meditation is— being still and listening to God. I don't think it makes much difference if we use a mantra or not. Personally, when I meditate I start off with a lesson from the Workbook, which I repeat over and over in my mind and then I switch to the mantra *Om*. Despite my difficulty with meditation, I have received some guidance while meditating. Occasionally a few words or a phrase will penetrate my mind. One such example is the following phrase, *"Life becomes a spiritual practice."* As soon as I came out of my meditation I wrote it down. It was obviously good advice. *"Where there is fear, there is no love or light"* was another message I once received during meditation. Yet another recent meditation in particular stands out in my mind. I heard a sudden bang and then saw a flash of light, like the flash on a camera. Then I clearly heard the words, *"I am everywhere."* I came out of the meditation rather annoyed because I thought it was the ego talking to me. Then, after some thought, I realised it was more likely to be a message from my higher self or the Holy Spirit and the message made sense. If we are all one and are all part of God, God is everywhere.

On another occasion when I was meditating on Lesson 14, *"God did not create a meaningless world,"* I heard the following: *"God did not create the thought that created a meaningless world."* I thought that was quite interesting because it was a reminder that our world was created by a thought—by the thought of the "wrong" portion of the split mind, which decided to try to live without God and therefore brought the ego and the universe into being, as I mentioned in Chapter 1. It is amazing how creative thoughts can be. It is also quite alarming because it means we have to be very careful about what we focus on in our minds. I believe if we focus on fear, we will attract fearful situations into our lives and therefore we have to try hard to avoid having any worrying or fear-inducing thoughts or memories.

One morning, when I was half awake and half asleep I received a clear image

---

[316] *ACIM*, W225, Lesson 125.

in my mind of a medium-sized delivery van. Written in large letters on the sides of the van was the word, *"Miracles."* I didn't really understand the significance but maybe I was supposed to be delivering miracles to other people? Maybe miracles are the most important thing we can give each other. If we recall that a miracle is a changed perception of the world, a correction of our erroneous way of thinking, the replacement of illusions with truth and the replacement of attack with forgiveness, then what could be more important?

I sometimes receive guidance through dreams. I remember one recent dream that made me very happy. I dreamt a nurse was performing an operation on my stomach to remove something. Whilst she was doing that, I was simultaneously in another part of the building, dealing with people, working, etc. The reason I was pleased when I woke up was that I had actually managed, for the first time, to identify with my spirit rather than with my body. The "I" that I felt was me, was the person who was working and dealing with others. I was not the body that was being operated upon. I have had a few premonitory dreams as well, but the trouble with dreams is that they are not consistently reliable. Some make sense but others seem to be totally daft!

I was watching a demonstration on television one day and the banner read, *"We Want Freedom."* Everybody wants freedom I thought to myself but maybe we don't really know from what. It appears to us that we need freedom from a country that is acting aggressively towards us, or is occupying us; or freedom from the mundane routine of going to work every day (hence we may try our luck on the lottery); or freedom from an unhappy relationship; or freedom of speech, etc. It's a long and valid list but I can't help thinking that what we really want, and are unaware of, is freedom from the ego. We want to be released from its clutches and return to the ultimate freedom we had before the separation when we were one with God. I think this subconscious urge is behind all the demands for all the various types of freedoms that people call for here on earth.

I have always been a freedom lover myself and that was why I could not stay married for very long, even though my husband was a wonderful person. I just had this strong urge to be totally unattached and totally free and this is how I have remained ever since—for over 25 years. When I am stuck in my office at work which, as I have mentioned, does not have an external window, I often feel trapped and I look forward to end of the work day when I can walk home across a large, open green field. I always heave a sigh of relief when I get to it. In fact, I think the claustrophobia that I suffer from is part my desire to be free and it may stem from a subconscious need to be free *from the ego.*

During the course of writing this book I have had the good fortune to read quite a few Buddhist and Hindu scriptures and one thing I noticed is that, whilst reading them, I felt very uplifted and happy. It was as though I was taken to another plane of existence. The ego vanishes when one focuses on the words of truth, as do all the petty worries and concerns of daily life. I always notice that all the silly little things that concern my ego seem to disappear whilst I am reading these lofty words. Could it be that these ancient scriptures give off a sort of energy that is picked up by the reader? Many times I have felt like typing up the various scriptures and having them framed on my bedroom wall. Anyway, I hope the reader of this book feels the same way when he reads these ancient texts. I must add that the same can be said about the words of *ACIM*. Every night I look forward to reading a few pages of the *Course*, or a few passages, depending on how sleepy I am, because this *always* inspires me and it is a wonderful way to put the worries of the day aside just before sleeping.

I think being positive and cheerful is so important, especially in the current world situation, with all the gloom and doom we are bombarded with via the radio, the television and the Internet. I know life can be a struggle and it isn't always easy to be joyful. I remember when I first started teaching how difficult it was to pay all the bills and raise my son on my own. I don't know how I did it, but I used to travel into London, work all day, then come home, do the household chores and give private lessons in the evening and during the weekend. I would not have been able to survive if I hadn't done this. But through it all I usually managed to remain cheerful and optimistic. An Indian sage once said that negativity is as contagious as a cold and that if one is in a bad mood one should not have the right to go out in public and pass the "germ" on to others!

Talking of optimism, I have a good but rather pessimistic friend whom I chat to occasionally on the phone. One day we were discussing the meaning of life when she said, *"If you think about it, the moment one is born one is on a journey to the grave."* I had to agree with her, but there is another, much more optimistic way, of looking at it. Instead of thinking that every day brings you closer to your grave, and I am sure this is quite a common thought amongst the elderly, say to yourself instead, *"Everyday that goes by brings me one day closer to enlightenment."* Now that is a cheering thought. That's what life is all about—enlightenment—even if society and the media believe otherwise. So as I look in the mirror and notice a new wrinkle, although it isn't exactly pleasing, I think that maybe, just maybe, as I grow old I will grow up too and become more mature from the spiritual point of view. I think aspiration is very important. Unless we really and truly desire to reach salvation, we won't stand a chance.

Even though I find the teaching of *ACIM* to be inspiring and uplifting, I must be honest and admit that very occasionally I feel rather dejected. This is because I now accept what the *Course* is saying but therefore feel trapped. I am aware that this world is an illusion, but I am not so sure that I will find my way out of it. Is there really any means of escape? I often open *ACIM* at random and ask for advice from the Holy Spirit. Strangely enough one evening, when I was feeling rather gloomy about it all, I did just that and I came across the following passage: *"You may wonder how you can be at peace when, while you are in time, there is so much that must be done before the way to peace is open. Perhaps this seems impossible to you. But ask yourself if it is possible that God would have a plan for your salvation that does not work. Once you accept His plan as the one function that you would fulfil, there will be nothing else the Holy Spirit will not arrange for you without your effort. He will go before you making straight your path, and leaving in your way no stones to trip on, and no obstacles to bar your way. Nothing you need will be denied you. Not one seeming difficulty but will melt away before you reach it...."* [317] This certainly boosted my morale because now I know God *has* a plan for our salvation and there *is* a way out even if it isn't apparent to me right now. The way the *Course* suggests is to follow the Holy Spirit, practice forgiveness at every step of the way and point the way to others so that they too can awaken from the dream. I really hope this book has helped some readers and encouraged them to either become an *ACIM* student themselves or to find a path Home that suits them better.

In both Hinduism and Buddhism, the Path to God consists of the belief in

---

[317] *ACIM*, T433 & 434.

non-duality and the need to practice contemplation, meditation, prayer, purity, non-violence, non-attachment, compassion and altruism. These are not really all that different from the Path according to *ACIM*. The latter also stresses non-duality or non-separation but it also teaches us that forgiveness is the way Home. It says as well that we need to be still and quiet in order to hear the voice of the Holy Spirit. And it emphasises the need to be non-judgemental and to never attack another being (neither verbally nor physically.) Thus non-violence can be seen as being part of the teachings of the *Course*. Non-attachment is also implied in *ACIM*, which denies the existence of the physical body. How can we attach ourselves to material possessions and to our bodies, if they don't really exist, even if they appear to? Although prayers are not really central to the teachings of the *Course*, a number of lovely prayers are given in the Workbook. Mantras and the recitation of holy scriptures play a large part in Hinduism and Buddhism. In *ACIM* affirmations are given throughout the Workbook, which could be used in the same way as mantras during moments of contemplation and meditation. One of my favourite ones is the following: *"I am not a body, I am free. For I am still as God created me."* [318]

Right understanding plays a part in all three belief systems. The first path of Buddha's *Eightfold Noble Path* is *right understanding* or *right view*. True knowledge and discernment play a large part in jnana yoga, which is the yoga of knowledge. As Ramana Maharshi, the Indian philosopher and teacher of the *Advaita Vedanta*, said, *"Non-attachment combined with Self-knowledge wins the kingdom of deliverance. Non-attachment and knowledge are like the wings of a bird needed for ascending the mount of deliverance, and if either of them is lacking it cannot be attained."* [319] And *ACIM* teaches us that we have to switch from using the "wrong" portion of the mind, which is controlled by the ego, to using the "right" portion, which is under the direction of the Holy Spirit. Before we can really do this, we have to study the 365 lessons in the Workbook. In fact, it takes a lot of study and contemplation to absorb the teachings of the Text, Workbook and Manual of *ACIM*. It cannot be done without the use of the logical mind, even though eventually one will have

---

[318] *ACIM*, W388, Lesson 201.

[319] Ramana Maharshi and Shankara, *Ramana, Shankara and the Forty Verses, The Essential Teachings of Advaita*, p. 53, Watkins Publishing, London 2002.

to transcend it. So in all three belief systems once again we can draw a parallel.

The Buddha told his disciples, *"I am awake."* I think he meant, by this statement, that he understood the true nature of the self and that the world of phenomena was not real. Awakening from the dream forms a central part of the teachings of *ACIM*. This means we need to have true self-knowledge. We need to know that we are *not* the ego or the body that was "miscreated" by the ego. We need to know that our true self is spirit, united with Christ and God. We need to realise that it's all an illusion.

As for the physical body, some of the Hindu and Buddhist texts I have studied deny the existence of the physical body and the world of phenomena. Others deny the reality of the ego but do not deal with the issue of the reality or non-reality of the physical body. But what nearly all these teachings have in common is the recognition that *we are not our bodies or our egos*. Hindus believe that we are the divine essence within the body, i.e., soul or spirit. Buddhists believe that *cause and effect* are responsible for our apparent existence in the physical world. *ACIM* states that we *are* spirit but we are *not* the spirit that dwells in the body. The body is unreal but only appears to be real. The *Course totally denies* the existence of the ego and the physical body. *"God did not make the body, because it is destructible, and therefore not of the Kingdom. The body is the symbol of what you think you are. It is clearly a separation device, and therefore does not exist."* [320]

Other thinkers and philosophers have realised that we are more than just our physical bodies, all separate from each other. Albert Einstein was one of them. He also said that our beliefs about ourselves were restrictive. *"A human being is part of the whole called by us universe, a part limited in time and space. We experience ourselves, our thoughts and feelings as something separate from the rest. A kind of optical delusion of consciousness. This delusion is a kind of prison for us, restricting us to our personal desires and to affection for a few persons nearest to us. Our task must be to free ourselves from the prison by widening our circle of compassion to embrace all living creatures and the whole of nature in its beauty. The true value of a human being is determined by the measure and the sense in which they have obtained liberation from the*

---

[320] *ACIM,* T105.

self. We shall require a substantially new manner of thinking if humanity is to survive." [321]

That was a quotation I came across on the website www.spaceandmotion.com. It was explained on that website that, although humans appear to be separate individuals, in reality all matter, which includes humans, consists of *"wave structures of the universe,"* and we vibrate or resonate with everything in the space around us. We are all interconnected to all other matter, even the stars in the sky. Thus, *"Seeing our bodies as discrete and separate objects is an illusion of our limited senses (as representations of the mind.)"*

David Hawkins, whom I mentioned earlier, described one of his enlightenment experiences like this: *"In the motionless Silence, it became obvious that there are no 'events' or 'things' and that nothing actually 'happens' because past, present, and future are merely artifacts of perception, as is the illusion of a separate 'I' being subject to birth and death. As the limited, false self dissolved into the universal Self of its true origin, there was an ineffable sense of having returned home to a state of absolute peace and relief from all suffering. It is only the illusion of individuality that is the origin of all suffering."* [322] Yet again we see that individuality is referred to as an illusion. In fact, that last sentence is exactly what the *Course* says with reference to the ego. Individuality and multiplicity are the creations of the ego and they are not real. They are also the cause of our suffering in this illusory world, where everything is transitory and inevitably ends in decay and death. When we return to our original state we will experience, as David Hawkins did, a sense of complete oneness with God and His creations. We will be absorbed back into the *"universal Self"* mentioned in this passage.

Describing how he actually managed to achieve that enlightened state of awareness, David Hawkins said that he had a very intense desire to reach it; he was also compassionate towards others and towards himself and he acted with *"constant and universal forgiveness and gentleness, without exception."* [323] He also said

---

[321] http://www.spaceandmotion.com/albert-einstein-god-religion-theology.htm.

[322] David Hawkins, *Discovery of the Presence of God – Devotional Nonduality*, p. 287, Veritas Publishing, Arizona 2006.

[323] Ibid., p. 292.

he kept all desires under control and turned them over to God. In this way he was able to transcend the chattering of his mind and experience the *"Silence,"* as he called it.

Now let's turn to the topic of miracles. In the previous chapter I mentioned how miracles can shift time and save *"thousands of years"* of hard work in terms of spiritual evolution. Miracles also have a great healing power because they change our perceptions so that we no longer feel separate either from God or from others. We realise we are joined with them and this heals us from all the fear and guilt that originated at the time of the separation millions of years ago. *"That you and your brother are joined is your salvation; the gift of Heaven, not the gift of fear."* [324] We come across the same idea in Lesson 95 of the Workbook. *"I am one Self, united with my Creator, at one with every aspect of creation, and limitless in power and in peace."* That is an incredibly powerful statement. The lesson goes on to explain that our one goal is to bring the awareness of this oneness to *all* minds. So all *Course* students, who really make an effort to understand and practice the teachings and try to explain them to others, are fulfilling their divine purpose. This could be done during discussions with friends, in workshops, through books or periodicals, through the Internet and through social gatherings. I don't think the method matters too much. What matters is that we help others to awaken from the nightmare of the ego. I am aware that we may encounter disbelief and derision, when we do so. But that should not deter us. Those who are ready for the teachings of the *Course* will prick up their ears and listen. Those who are not must have the freedom to walk away. Maybe they will find another path back Home.

The following extremely bleak picture that is painted of the world of the ego should be enough to encourage anyone to awaken. *"Real choice is not illusion. But the world has none to offer. All its roads but lead to disappointment, nothingness and death. There is no choice in its alternatives. Seek not escape from problems here. The world was made that problems could not **be** escaped. Be not deceived by all the different names its roads are given. They have but one end....On some you travel gaily for a while,*

---

[324] *ACIM*, T460.

before the bleakness enters. And on some the thorns are felt at once. The choice is not what will the ending be, but when it comes." [325] How true that is. If you stop to think about it for a moment you will agree that all roads in our world lead to nothingness and death. But I think it is because we have many years of enjoyment before this realisation (at least some of us do), that we do not really appreciate the futility of our existence. At a very young age I pondered upon the purpose of life. I couldn't understand it. What is the purpose of growing up, growing old, growing sick and dying? What does it mean? Finally I now realise that it doesn't mean anything. It is all a fabrication of the ego. And we can't blame God because *"God did not create a meaningless world."* [326]

ACIM states quite bluntly that if we see ourselves as flesh, we will never escape or never become enlightened. Actually the word "enlightenment" is not used very much in the *Course*— the word "salvation" is used instead. *"You see the flesh or recognize the spirit. There is no compromise between the two. If one is real the other must be false, for what is real denies its opposite...If you choose flesh, you never will escape the body as your own reality, for you have chosen that you want it so. But choose the spirit, and all Heaven bends to touch your eyes and bless your holy sight, that you may see the world of flesh no more except to heal and comfort and to bless."* [327]

Yet despite the warning in this passage, we are told that enlightenment or salvation is not that difficult. *"Think not the way to Heaven's gate is difficult at all. Nothing you undertake with certain purpose and high resolve and happy confidence, holding your brother's hand and keeping step to Heaven's song, is difficult to do."* [328] It is precisely passages like this that encourage me to keep going and give me hope for salvation. Keeping step to Heaven's song means following the guidance of the Holy Spirit, Who is our teacher as we walk towards Heaven. But you will note that we are not supposed to walk alone for we must take others there with us.

---

[325] *ACIM,* T653.
[326] *ACIM,* W23, Lesson 14.
[327] *ACIM,* T660.
[328] *ACIM,* T550.

Nevertheless, we must not underestimate the amount of work or time it could take for us to achieve salvation. *Course* teacher Kenneth Wapnick explains, *"Obviously, within our dream of time, it appears as if it will take a tremendous amount of time for sin to be undone and our minds healed....When we consider our individual egos and how long it will take to be totally free on that level, and then multiply that a billion-fold in terms of the world at large, the end of the ego would seem to be a long, long way off."* But then he explains that this way of looking at it reinforces the illusion of time. What we need to understand is that all we have to do is to change our perception of the world. *"All that is needed for the world of time to disappear for us as reality is to change our minds, to 'change channels'."* [329] So in terms of our linear perception of time, salvation could be a long way away *unless* we decide to go for it right now.

One of my favourite wise men, Wei Wu Wei, also believed that satori (enlightenment) could be a very slow process. *"But there is not, never was and never could be, anything sudden about satori except the event itself, i.e., the 'turning-over (paravritti) of the mind—and that is necessarily instantaneous—a seizure of the present. Its preparation may be considered to require untold millions of our years...."* [330] What he is saying is that, although the actual experience of enlightenment can happen in a flash (which is what David Hawkins said, as we saw in Chapter 2), there could be millions of years of preparatory work before that experience. So it doesn't make much sense to waste yet another lifetime.

I would like to mention something that I haven't dealt with before—the *"real world."* In *ACIM* this signifies a world in which the ego has been conquered and where love has taken the place of fear. It is experienced by those who have learnt all their forgiveness lessons and who have become truly awake. They could then be described as being, "in this world but not of it." It is a stage *before* salvation but it is a place of peace and a place where time no longer has any purpose. *"The real world cannot be perceived except through eyes forgiveness blesses, so they see a world where terror is impossible, and witnesses to fear can not be found...The real world*

---

[329] Kenneth Wapnick, *A Vast Illusion—Time according to A Course in Miracles*, pp. 222-223, Temecula, California, 2006, used by permission of the Foundation for A Course in Miracles.

[330] Wei Wu Wei, *Fingers Pointing towards the Moon*, p. 122, First Sentient Publications, Colorado, USA, 2003.

is the symbol that the dream of sin and guilt is over, and God's Son no longer sleeps." [331]

Salvation follows closely in the wake of those who have managed to attain the real world. Now God takes *"His final step"* and we are liberated. *"And as we look upon a world forgiven, it is He Who calls to us and comes to take us home, reminding us of our Identity which our forgiveness has restored to us."* [332]

Now seems like the right time to mention the Last Judgement. It is not the time when God judges us and casts us away either in heaven or in hell. It follows the Second Coming which, as I mentioned earlier on in this book, is the time when *all of us* have undone our egos and are able to live in the real world. We have collectively followed the guidance of the Holy Spirit and He has led us Home. (Or we have found another way Home.) The Last Judgement then is the end of the world of form. It is not a fearful experience because at this point we return to our source, Heaven. *"The final judgment on the world contains no condemnation. For it sees the world as totally forgiven, without sin and wholly purposeless. Without a cause, and now without a function in Christ's sight, it merely slips away to nothingness....And all the figures in the dream in which the world began go with it. Bodies now are useless, and will therefore fade away, because the Son of God is limitless."* [333] This is not a frightening experience because we will have no need for bodies, or for the earth or for any other aspect of the illusion. We will be spirit as we were when God created us and we will all be joined, one with each other and one with God.

Why is our salvation or enlightenment inevitable? Because, according to the metaphysics of the *Course*, it has already happened. In reality there is no time or space and we are where we always were—in Heaven. But from the perspective of the ego, we are not in Heaven. We are living in this physical world, a place of refuge that it created for our bodies. What we are really doing is reliving, over and over again, the initial moment of separation from God. Kenneth Wapnick describes this so well in his wonderful book *A Vast Illusion—Time according to A Course in Miracles*. It's the sort of book one has to read several times because it

---

[331] *ACIM,* W443.
[332] *ACIM,* W443.
[333] *ACIM,* W455.

sheds so much light on a rather abstruse topic. Each time you re-read it, you learn more.

I am aware that I have used the term "achieve enlightenment" several times in this book and that this term is not strictly correct because enlightenment is not something to be achieved. It is our natural state. What we need to achieve is the realisation that we are, in fact, already enlightened, as we were before the separation (which didn't actually take place.) It is rather complicated but, according to both Buddhism and *ACIM*, *illumination* cannot be realised because we possess it already. It is not an object to be found; it is our nature or the nature of the One Mind, which is all that exists. The greatest impediment that we have to overcome is ignorance and the ego is responsible for our ignorance. So it would be more accurate to use the terms *awakening from the illusion (or dream)* or realising *our true nature* instead of *achieving enlightenment* or *attaining liberation*.

Kenneth Wapnick explains this quite clearly when he speaks about the resurrection, *"Thus, the resurrection has already happened within us; it simply awaits our acceptance of this fact...Because there is no linear time, each and every seeming instant within the observer's mind offers the opportunity of being free from the prison of the past. In truth there is no past; we have no history, personal or collective."* [334] He goes on to explain that either we choose the ego and remain trapped in time and space, or we choose to follow the Holy Spirit and forgive others and ourselves. That is the path to salvation.

ACIM explains clearly that salvation is inevitable because God has promised it to us. *"Salvation is a promise, made by God, that you would find your way to Him at last. It cannot but be kept."* [335] Right at the end of the *Course* we come across the same message but are warned that doubts may arise in our minds at times. *"Forget not once this journey is begun the end is certain. Doubt along the way will come and go and go to come again. Yet is the ending sure. No one can fail to do what God appointed him to do."* [336] I am sure many *Course* students experience feelings of

---

[334] Kenneth Wapnick, *A Vast Illusion — Time according to A Course in Miracles*, p. 65, Temecula, California, 2006, used by permission of the Foundation for A Course in Miracles.

[335] *ACIM*, W407.

[336] *ACIM*, Clarification of Terms, p. 91.

doubt from time to time. I know I do. I think I am doubtful at times because I am impatient. I want to awaken *now*, but that's not how it happens. But by re-reading *ACIM* I rise above any doubts that the ego has managed to slip into my mind. How could I doubt when I read words like, *"The end **is** sure and guaranteed by God."* And further on, on the same page, *"Long ago the end was written in the stars and set into the Heavens with a shining Ray that held it safe within eternity and through all time as well. And holds it still; unchanged, unchanging and unchangeable. Be not afraid. We only start again an ancient journey long ago begun that but seems new....We had lost our way but He has found it for us...."* [337] How can we doubt, when we have Christ as our teacher and guide?

Lesson 292 assures us of our success. *"A happy outcome to all things is sure. God's promises make no exceptions. And He guarantees that only joy can be the final outcome found for everything. Yet it is up to us when this is reached; how long we let an alien will* (the ego's will) *appear to be opposing His...."* Clearly the choice is ours. For me there is no choice, because I have decided that enough is enough. I have been procrastinating for lifetime after lifetime, I am sure of that. Now something or someone is calling out to me and I must respond. And I am reminded of this each time I read Lesson 226 of the Workbook: *"My home awaits me. I will hasten there."*

The following passage, one of the most beautiful in the *Course*, reminds me of what is in store for me, and for all of us, when we finally awaken. *"Beyond the body, beyond the sun and stars, past everything you see and yet somehow familiar, is an arc of golden light that stretches as you look into a great shining circle. And all the circle fills with light before your eyes. The edges of the circle disappear, and what is in it is no longer contained at all. The light expands and covers everything, extending to infinity forever shining and with no break or limit anywhere. Within it everything is joined in perfect continuity. Nor is it possible to imagine that anything could be outside, for there is nowhere that this light is not."* [338]

So it is really down to us. Do we really want to carry on dreaming as we have been doing for aeons? Or do we recognise the illusion of life on earth and decide to awaken from the dream and return Home? We all do so much travelling these

---

[337] *ACIM*, Clarification of Terms, p. 91 & 92.
[338] *ACIM*, T447.

days. We go to different places and new countries every year in search of adventure or sunshine or leisure. But the time will come when we realise that the only worthwhile journey is the one back Home. And, we are told, it isn't really a journey at all. It is simply a matter of awakening from the dream. Do you feel the time is right for you?

Lightning Source UK Ltd.
Milton Keynes UK
UKOW07f0001200617

303658UK00002B/281/P